P. 8

To The
TOWN'S TASTE
1937

PRESS OF THE FREDONIA CENSOR

WIRE-O BINDING. PATENTS PENDING

ROCHESTER WIRE-O BINDING CO., LICENSEES

To The
TOWN'S TASTE

SIGNED RECIPES

Published By

THE WESTMINSTER CLUB

of the

FIRST PRESBYTERIAN CHURCH

Fredonia, New York

1937

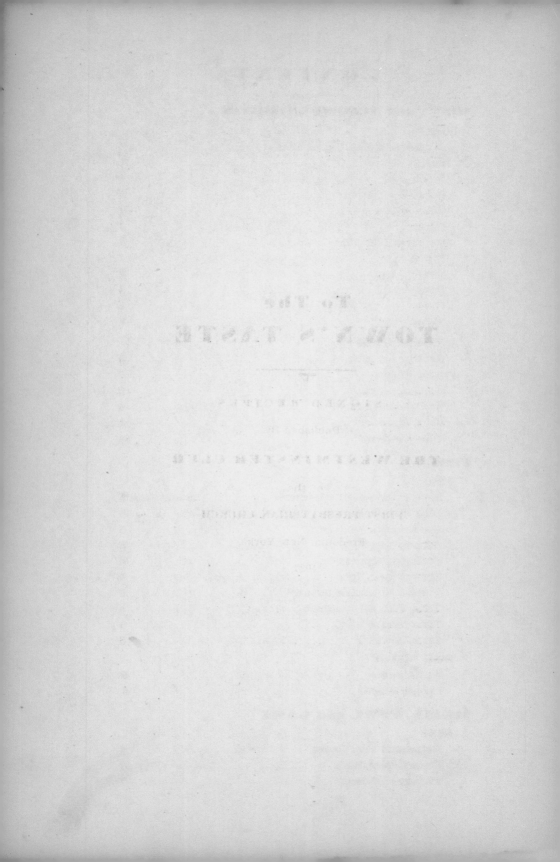

CONTENTS

SOUPS and ACCOMPANIMENTS . . .

EGGS, CHEESE and CASSEROLE DISHES

VEGETABLES

SALADS and DRESSINGS

SALAD DRESSINGS

SALADS

BREADS

BREADS MADE WITH YEAST

ROLLS

COFFEE CAKES WITH YEAST

BAKING POWDER BREADS

COFFEE CAKES WITH BAKING POWDER

HOT BREADS, WAFFLES, GRIDDLE CAKES, ETC.

CAKES and ICINGS

CAKES

ICINGS AND FILLINGS

COOKIES and DOUGHNUTS

COOKIES

DESSERTS

PIES

ICE BOX PUDDINGS AND CAKES

PUDDINGS

PICKLES and RELISHES

PICKLES

RELISHES

MISCELLANEOUS

SANDWICHES

CHILDREN'S RECIPES

HOUSEHOLD HINTS

SUBSTITUTIONS
and
EQUIVALENTS

◆

1 tablespoon flour equals ½ tablespoon cornstarch, equals ½ tablespoon quick cooking tapioca.

1 ounce chocolate equals 3 tablespoons cocoa plus ½ tablespoon fat.

1⅓ cups brown sugar equals 1 cup white granulated sugar.

¼ teaspoon soda plus 1 cup sour milk equals 1 teaspoon baking powder plus 1 cup sweet milk.

1 teaspoon baking powder equals ¼ teaspoon soda plus ½ teaspoon cream of tartar.

1 tablespoon fresh grated horseradish equals 2 tablespoons bottled.

1 cup molasses equals ½ cup sugar plus ¼ cup liquid.

2 cups butter equals 1 pound.

4 tablespoons flour equals 1 ounce.

4 cups flour equals 1 pound.

1 cup pearl tapioca equals ¾ cup quick-cooking tapioca.

2 cups granulated sugar equals 1 pound.

2½ to 3 cups powdered sugar equals 1 pound.

2⅔ cups brown sugar equals 1 pound.

2 tablespoons liquid equals 1 ounce.

2 tablespoons butter equals 1 ounce.

3½ cups walnuts (chopped) equals 1 pound.

Kedgeree

1 cup boiled white fish (flaked)
1 cup boiled rice
2 hard boiled eggs
  Seasoning to taste

Mix all ingredients together and serve hot. The hard boiled eggs are, of course, chopped and added. If one likes the mixture a little moist, milk may be added.

Eleanor Roosevelt

SOUPS . . .

Standard Recipe for All Cream Soups

Vegetable or meat stock	2 cups milk
2 rounding tablespoons flour	1 teaspoon salt
2 rounding tablespoons butter	½ teaspoon pepper

1. Melt butter and stir in flour.   2. Add milk, salt and pepper.   3. Cook in double boiler.   4. Add 2 cups of any vegetable or meat stock and blend together. Serves 6.

PUREES

Puree is made by adding the pulp of cooked vegetables to milk or cream. The milk is thickened with flour or corn starch in order to bind the solid and liquid parts together. Puree is generally thicker than cream soup. Stock may be added.

Mary E. Smith

BLACK BEAN SOUP

1 cup black beans	1 bay leaf
2 ounces salt pork	½ teaspoon salt
1 small onion	¼ teaspoon pepper
1 carrot, diced	1 teaspoon lemon juice
2 stalks celery	1 lemon sliced
1 whole clove	1 hard cooked egg, sliced
½ teaspoon dry mustard	Water

1. Cover beans with water and soak over night. Drain.   2. Dry out salt pork, add onion. When slightly browned add carrot, celery, clove, mustard, bay leaf, salt and pepper. 3. Simmer until beans are soft, replenishing water as it boils off. It will require from three to four hours to cook beans.   4. Rub through a sieve. Add more water (boiling) if necessary and reheat. Just before serving add lemon juice.   5. Garnish with egg and lemon. — Serves 6.

Lois M. Thompson

BORSTCH (RUSSIAN)

6 large beets	2 eggs
Juice of ½ lemon	1 pint sour cream
1 tablespoon sugar	

1. Peel beets, grate coarsely or dice.   2. Cover beets with water, add salt to taste. Boil until beets are tender. 3. Add lemon juice and sugar, let cool. When slightly warm, beat eggs and add beet soup to the eggs. Mix well.   4. Do not have the soup too warm or eggs will curdle.   5. Place in refrigerator. When ready to use mix 1 pint sour cream to the beet mixture.
Hot boiled potatoes may be served with this soup.

Mrs. Harry Ballotin

CLAM BROTH

1 pint clams   Salt
1 quart milk   Paprika
1 tablespoon butter

1. Pick over the clams.   2. Add 1 cup water and simmer 8 minutes.   3. Add milk and seasoning.

Mrs. J. C. Boody

CORN SOUP

2 cups corn (canned or fresh)   2 tablespoons butter
1 cup boiling water   2 tablespoons flour
3 cups milk   Salt and pepper
1 tablespoon grated onion

1. Melt butter in top of double boiler.   2. Stir in the flour until creamy. 3. Add milk and seasoning.   4. Add corn and heat thoroughly.   5. Corn may be put through a sieve if preferred.

Esther Rabin

CREAM OF TOMATO SOUP

1 pint canned tomatoes   2 tablespoons flour
1 pint milk   1 small onion
½ pint water   ½ teaspoon soda
2 tablespoons butter   Salt and pepper

1. Stew tomatoes and onions together until onion is tender.   2. Run pulp through a sieve.   3. Heat milk, thicken with paste made of flour and butter. 4. Add soda to tomatoes, stir well and gradually pour in the milk.   5. Add salt and pepper to taste.

Marguerite F. Britz

ONION SOUP

2 quarts meat broth   2 tablespoons butter
6 medium sized onions   Salt and pepper

1. Slice onions thin, brown in butter and add to broth.   2. Add seasoning and simmer until onions are tender.   Serve hot.
Croutons sprinkled with grated cheese slightly melted under the broiler may be served with the soup.

Esther Rabin

POTATO SOUP

4 medium sized potatoes   2 tablespoons flour
1 quart milk   Salt and pepper
1 small onion, diced   1 teaspoon chopped celery
3 tablespoons butter

1. Cook potatoes until tender. Rub through a sieve.   2. Scald milk with onion and add to potato, stirring constantly. 3. Melt butter, add seasoning and cook over slow fire.

Esther Rabin

SAUER SOUP

2 pounds pork loin
2 cups finely cubed carrots
2 cups cut green beans

2 cups diced potatoes
2 tablespoons sugar
½ cup vinegar

1. Cook pork in plenty of salted water until nearly done. 2. Add carrots, beans and potatoes. Boil until tender. 3. Add sugar and vinegar and let stand ten minutes before serving.

Edna Foss

OYSTER SOUP

1 quart milk (top or whole)
1 quart oysters
1 small onion
1 stalk celery

1 large tablespoon butter
1 heaping teaspoon flour
1 cup finely rolled cracker
crumbs

1. Put milk, celery, onion into double boiler and let boil until onion and celery can be tasted in milk. 2. Put oysters in pan and heat through. 3. Melt butter and stir in flour until smooth. 4. Strain celery and onion out of milk. Add butter and flour mixture. Be careful there are no lumps. 5. Salt and pepper to taste. 6. Add 1 teaspoon Worcestershire sauce. 7. Pour in oysters. and let cook until edges curl. 8. Just before serving, add cracker crumbs.

Mrs. Gerald Williams

SCOTCH BROTH (From a Scotch Family)

1 large beef shank
Cold water to cover
1 small white turnip
Put all through the food chopper
1 can telephone peas
1 cup pearl barley

2 medium carrots
¼ head kale or cabbage
4 large leeks or onions

1 cup rice

Salt and pepper to taste. Cook all together slowy, except peas which are added just before serving. May be kept in a cold place and reheated as needed.

Mrs. Daniel A. Reed
(*From the Congressional Cookbook*)

NOODLES FOR SOUP

Flour
1 tablespoon cold water

1 egg
Pinch of salt

1. Mix enough flour with the beaten egg and water until the dough is very stiff. 2. Mix well and roll as thin as possible. 3. Let dry a few minutes, cut into strips. 4. Place on moulding board until thoroughly dry. 5. Drop into boiling broth and let boil just a few minutes.

Mrs. L. S. Foley, Dunkirk

CHOWDERS ...

GLOUCESTER FISH CHOWDER

4 pounds Cod or Haddock
1 quart sliced potatoes
½ pound salt pork, diced
1 onion sliced thin
4 cups boiling water

2 cups milk
(more may be added)
2 tablespoons flour
1 tablespoon butter
Salt and pepper

1. Remove skin and bones from fish and cut into small pieces. Season each piece with salt and pepper.   2. Parboil potatoes 8 minutes and drain.   3. Fry salt pork until crisp.   4. Add onion to pork and cook until yellow.   5. Put fish, then potatoes in kettle in layers with the pork and onion on each layer. Add 4 cups boiling water and cook on top of stove until fish is done.   6. Melt butter in a pan, add flour, then milk stirring until smooth.   7. Pour this into the chowder when cooked and serve with split crackers.   8. More milk may be added if thinner chowder is desired.

Mrs. Daniel Harmon

NEW ENGLAND CLAM CHOWDER

½ pound pork
2 large onions
5 large potatoes
1 pint of milk

2-3 can No. 2 tomatoes
1 5-ounce can clams
½ teaspoon salt
Pepper

1. Cube pork and fry golden brown. Add onions cut fine and brown carefully.
2. Cube and boil tender the potatoes in just enough water to cover.   3. Add 1 pint of milk. When this simmers add the juice from clams.   4. Pull clams into small pieces leaving the stomachs whole and add to the mixture.   5. Add the pork, onions, salt and pepper.   6. When this reaches a boil, add tomatoes. Let simmer very slowly 1 hour or more. Serve with Pilot Biscuits.

Mrs. B. H. Ritenburg

CLAM CHOWDER

1½ dozen clams
½ pound bacon
6 carrots
2-3 medium onions
4 medium potatoes

2 bunches celery cut very fine
1 medium can tomatoes
1 small can peas
1 small can corn

1. Cut bacon in small pieces and fry crisp. 2. Add clams cut in small pieces using all fat and juice. 3. Cook 15 or 20 minutes. 4. Grind all vegetables except celery.   Add to clams.   Add canned vegetables and let simmer. Just before serving add a pinch of soda and ½ cup sweet cream. Season.

Abbie Walker

CORN CHOWDER

1 can Golden Bantam corn
2 cups diced potatoes
2 slices fat salt pork
1 onion, diced

1 quart milk
3 tablespoons butter
Salt
Pepper

1. Cut pork in small pieces and fry until crisp.   Remove from fat and save.
2. Add onion to fat and cook 5 minutes.   3. Parboil potatoes in water to cover for five minutes   4. Add this to onions and fat.   Cook until potatoes are soft.   5. Heat corn in milk. Add to potatoes, season with salt, pepper and butter.   6. Serve with pieces of crisped, salt pork scattered over individual servings.

Gladys M. Parker

FISH ...

BLUE PIKE IN BATTER

1 pint sour milk
1 yeast cake
1 egg

Salt
Flour to make batter
½ teaspoon soda

1. Crumble yeast cake in ¼ cup lukewarm water. 2. Beat egg well. 3. Add yeast mixture and milk, salt and flour to make batter. 4. Allow to stand 3 or 4 hours. 5. Mix soda with little warm water. Add just before using. 6. Dip fish in batter and fry in deep fat.

Mrs. Donald G. Seydel

NOODLE LUNCHEON DISH

½ pound noodles
1 can mushroom soup

1 can tuna or shrimp
Salt and pepper

1. Cook noodles in salted water until tender. 2. Drain and place in buttered casserole. Add either shrimp or tuna and pour mushroom soup over all. Add seasoning and bake 30 minutes in moderate oven.

Mrs. K. J. Easling

SALMON LOAF

1 can salmon (leave juice in)
1 large cup bread crumbs
Juice of 1 lemon

3 eggs beaten
4 tablespoons melted butter
Salt and pepper

1. Mix all together. 2. Pack in well greased tin cans leaving room to swell.
3. Put on cover and place in water and boil 1 hour.

Olive S. Rykert

SCALLOPED OYSTERS

1 pint oysters
4 tablespoons oyster liquor
2 tablespoons milk or cream
½ cup stale bread crumbs

½ cup melted butter
1 cup cracker crumbs
Salt and pepper

1. Mix bread and cracker crumbs stir in butter. 2. Put a thin layer in bottom of shallow buttered baking dish. 3. Cover with oysters and sprinkle with salt and pepper. 4. Add half of oyster liquor and milk or cream. Repeat and cover top with remaining crumbs. 5. Bake 30 minutes in hot oven 450 degrees F. 6. Never allow more than 2 layers of oysters if 3 layers are used the middle will be underdone.
Sprinkle each layer with mace or grated nutmeg if desired.

Mrs. Russell Lawrence, Dunkirk, N. Y.

SHRIMP & RICE

1 cup rice
6 tablespoons catsup
1 green pepper
1 pint cream

4 cans or 1 pound shrimp
1 tablespoon Worchestershire
sauce
1 tablespoon butter

1. Cook rice. 2. Clean shrimp. 3. Chop pepper fine. 4. Mix all together bake in casserole moderate oven for 30 minutes. — Serves 8.

Dorothy Sievert

TUNA FISH AND ASPARAGUS

Fill baking dish with alternate layers of tuna fish and asparagus adding cream sauce between each layer. Top with bread crumbs. Bake slowly one hour.

Mrs. E. W. Christoffers

TUNA FISH EN CASSEROLE

1 can tuna fish
¼ pound potato chips

1 can mushroom soup

1. Butter casserole, drain fish. 2. Place in casserole alternating with layers of potato chips. 3. Pour over soup, top with chips, cover and bake in moderate oven ½ hour. Do not salt.

Laura McKale

TUNA FISH SCALLOP

½ can tuna fish
1 cup cooked rice
½ pound cut mushrooms

2 pimentos
3 green peppers

1. Pour boiling water over the fish, then cold water and drain. 2. Cook mushrooms in butter 15 minutes. 3. Put mixture together and pour white sauce over it.

Jessie Hillman

TUNA NEWBERG

2 tablespoons butter
2 tablespoons flour
1 ½ cups milk
½ teaspoon salt
⅛ teaspoon pepper

⅛ teaspoon paprika
1 egg slightly beaten
½ teaspoon onion juice
2 tablespoons cooking sherry
1 small can tuna fish

1. To melted butter add flour with seasonings. 2. Stir until smooth add milk and egg slowly while stirring. 3. Boil two-minutes. Add onion juice and sherry. 4. Pour over tuna fish which has been arranged on toast. 5. Two tablespoons lemon juice may be substituted for the sherry.

Louise S. Butler

WHITE SAUCE

4 tablespoons butter
3 tablespoons flour

1 ½ cups milk
½ cup cream

Sprinkle cheese on top and brown in oven.

Jessie Hillman

TARTAR SAUCE

1 cup mayonnaise
2 small dill pickles
Few chopped chives

Sprigs of parsley
1 Teaspoon sugar
Paprika

1. Chop pickles and chives. 2. Onion juice may be used in place of chives. 3. Add sugar, stir and garnish with dash of paprika.

Ida Weaver

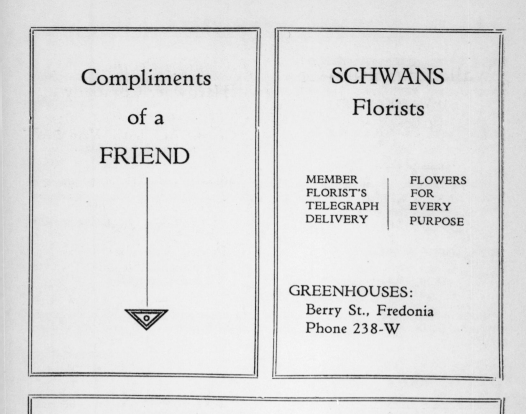

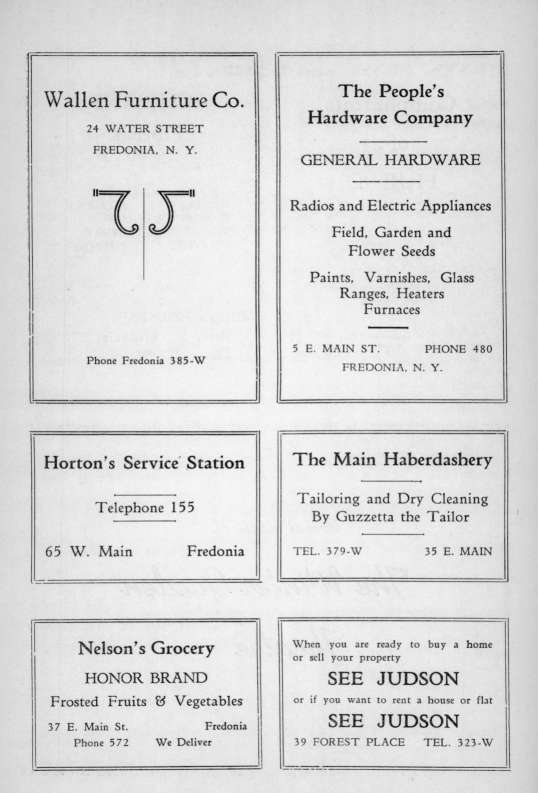

MEATS, FOWL and GAME . . .

BEEF . . .

BARBECUED BEEF ROAST

3 pounds beef rolled roast
Piece of suet
1 can tomato soup
1 green pepper
Salt and pepper

1 large onion
½ cup vinegar
1 teaspoon Worchestershire
sauce
2 bay leaves

1. Mix all ingredients. Place roast in this and allow to soak over night.
2. Roast as you would any meat. The sauce makes delicious gravy.

Mildred Rogger.

CORNED BEEF HASH

1 cup corned beef
2 cups potatoes
1 cup milk

¼ cup cream
Salt and pepper to taste

1. Chop meat and potatoes rather fine. Combine. 2. Put a heaping tablespoon butter in a frying pan, when it is melted but not browned, add potatoes, milk and meat, seasoning. 3. Cook for ½ hour, stirring, with a knife occasionally to prevent burning, but not enough to make it mushy. 4. Add cream and when it is thoroughly heated, remove it to a hot serving dish, with a cover.

Mrs. H. K. Williams, Dunkirk.

FRICASSEE OF BEEF

2 pounds chuck steak
1 large onion

½ cup catsup
Salt and pepper

1. Brown meat. 2. Cut onion, add cutsup and a little water. 3. Cook slowly about 2 hours, adding water as needed.

Mrs. Julia Waldron

MEAT BALLS

1 pound beef, ground
1 pound pork, ground
2 eggs

1 cup rolled cracker crumbs
1 small onion
Salt and pepper

1. Combine ingredients, roll in small balls. 2. Fry on hot griddle, allow to simmer 20 minutes. For meat loaf, add 1 cup milk and bake 1 hour.

Mrs. E. W. Schneider.

MEAT LOAF

1 pound hamburg
½ pound veal
½ pound salt pork
1 cup cracker crumbs

1 egg
Onion
1 cup milk
2 tomatoes

1. Combine ingredients and mix well. 2. Bake in moderate oven, 375o F. for 1 hour.

Inez M. Ransom.

MEAT LOAF

1½ pounds ground veal
½ pound fresh pork
2 eggs
2 cups milk

1 teaspoon salt
1 tablespoon sage
1 scant teaspoon pepper

1. Mix well and bake 2 to 3 hours, slowly.

Elizabeth S. Wolfe.

POT ROAST

4 pounds top round of beef or
4½ pounds chuck roast
1 can Campbells tomato soup

3 tablespoons vinegar
Worcestershire sauce
Salt and pepper

1. Brown beef on all sides in suet.   2. Remove meat from pan and pour off all but enough fat to brown onions.   3. Replace meat in pan and add other ingredients.   4. Bring to a boil, cover closely and simmer for 4 hours.   5. A heavy kettle or a Dutch oven is essential.   6. Remove meat and thicken gravy with 8 Zuzu's 'cookies' which have been softened in water.

Mrs. W. P. Sutherland Jr.

PRIME RIBS OF BEEF AU JUS

1. Either a rolled or standing roast of beef should be put in a hot oven, about 450 degrees F., for about 20 minutes, then turn oven to 400 to finish cooking.
2. Time required for rare beef is 20 minutes to the pound.   3. Never cover the roast, or it will steam. 4. If you wish to cook potatoes around the roast, put them in 1 hour before the required time for the roast to cook. 5. A few pieces of onion may be placed on top of the roast or the thinnest pieces of garlic in slits on the fatty part of the beef. Use only 1 clove of garlic.

Ida Weaver.

STEAK BARBECUE

1 ½ pounds ground round steak
¼ cup milk

Salt and pepper

1. Mix meat, milk and seasoning together.   2. Shape into patties.   3. Place on shallow dripping pan, ready for broiling.

BARBECUE SAUCE

¼ cup butter
2 tablespoons A-1 Sauce
1 teaspoon vinegar
Few drops Tobasco sauce

1 teaspoon sugar
2 tablespoons catsup
1 clove garlic, peeled

1. Put sauce ingredients in pan and simmer 5 minutes, to give garlic time to blend with other flavors. 2. Remove garlic.   3. Broil patties, basting with this hot sauce every few minutes.   4. Serve on rounds of buttered toast and pour gravy over patties.

Mary Heffernan, Dunkirk.

STEAK ROAST

1 thick steak
1 large green pepper
1 small onion

3 tablespoons tomato catsup
Butter
Salt and pepper

1. Place steak in pan and season with salt, pepper and butter.   2. Cover steak with sauce made of green pepper, chopped onion and catsup.   3. Add a little water and roast in hot oven for about 20 minutes.   4. Thicken the gravy left in pan and pour over steak when serving. Garnish with parsley.

Corinne L. Lounsberry.

SWISS STEAK SUPREME

2½ pounds round steack cut 1 inch thick	1 can peas
2 cans tomato soup	1 onion
	Salt, pepper and flour

1. Pound as much flour as possible into meat.   2. Place in baking dish and cover with tomato soup and equal amount of water.   3. Empty can of peas over meat and add onion and seasoning.   4. Cook in slow oven, for 2½ hours. 5. Potatoes may be added the last ¾ hours.   A complete dinner.

Mrs. K. J. Easling.

HAM . . .

HAM LOAF

1½ pounds fresh ham	1 cup soft bread crumbs
1½ pounds smoked ham	1 cup milk
	1 egg

1. Combine all ingredients and mix well.   2. Baste, while baking, with ½ cup brown sugar, 1 teaspoon dry mustard and 1½ cups diluted vinegar.

Marguerite Taft.

HAM ROLLS

1. Brush a slice of cold boiled ham with melted butter to which has been added a little mustard, pepper and salt.   2. Place 2 cooked asparagus tips, end to end, on ham and roll, fasten with toothpicks.   3. Place in moderate oven for 20 minutes or until heated through. Serve with cheese sauce.

Mrs. Jackson B. Clark

HAM AND VEAL LOAF

1 pound ground veal	¾ cup breadcrumbs
1 pound ground smoked ham	2 eggs
1 tablespoon minced onion	1 can mushroom soup
3 tablespoons green pepper	Salt and pepper
4 tablespoons catsup	

1. Combine ingredients and mix well.   2. Bake one hour — 350° F.

Mrs. M. H. Anderson.

UPSIDE DOWN HAM LOAF

1 pound ground ham	Red cherries
1½ pounds ground veal	2 eggs
½ pound ground fresh pork	2 cups soft bread crumbs
Pineapple slices	¼ cup milk

1. Mix meat, eggs, bread and milk together.   2. Melt a little butter and brown sugar in flat, shallow pan. 3. Completely cover bottom of pan with sliced pine-

apple with cherries in center of slice.   4. Cook until fruit is lightly brown on surface of range.   5. Cover with ham mixture and pat down evenly.   6. Bake in 355 degrees F. oven for 40 minutes.   7. Pour off surplus fat and juice and turn on platter.

Virginia Morrison.

LAMB ...

LAMB LOAF

2 pounds lamb (ground) use shoulder
1 cup milk
1 cup bread crumbs
1 tablespoon parsley

½ green pepper chopped
1 small onion
Salt and pepper
1 egg

1. Combine all ingredients.   2. Bake 1½ hours in a slow oven.

Mrs. C. F. Drewes, Dunkirk

PORK ...

DIXIE PORK CHOPS

6 pork chops
1-3 cup raisins
1 ½ tablespoons brown sugar

2 tablespoons vinegar
2 apples
Salt and pepper

1. Fry chops until brown, and place in deep dish.   2. Add flour and water to pan in which chops were browned to make gravy.   3. Add raisins, vinegar and brown sugar and pour over chops.   4. Peel and slice apples into thick slices and arrange on chops, and sprinkle with brown sugar.   5. Bake in moderate oven 45 minutes.

Carrie Slate.

HOME MADE SAUSAGE

4 pounds pork quite fat
1 pound beef
5 teaspoons powdered sage

5 teaspoons salt
1¾ teaspoons pepper

1. Have meat ground by butcher, or if done at home, grind twice or three times.
2. Mix seasoning through meat very thoroughly. The beef is added for body.

Helen Price Cowden.

VEAL ...

BREADED VEAL

1 loin of veal for each person
Egg

Buttered crumbs
Sour cream

1. Dip veal in egg, then buttered crumbs.   2. Fry slowly until light brown.
3. Place in roaster, partially cover with sour cream.   4. Bake slowly, covered, for 2 to 3 hours.   5. Serve with fried apple slices seasoned with cinnamon and brown sugar.

Elizabeth S. Wolfe.

DEVILED VEAL STEAK

1 pound veal cutlet, sliced ¼ inch thick
2 teaspoons prepared mustard
1 teaspoon salt

1 tablespoon butter
1 egg
2 cups rice flakes, (measured, then crumbed)

1. Cut steak into servings.   2. Mix mustard, salt, pepper and butter and rub into steak.   3. Dip in slightly beaten egg, then in rolled rice flakes and fry in skillet with a generous amount of hot fat.   4. Garnish with sliced tomatoes or pickle and serve with buttered green beans.

Gladys I. Stanley.

VEAL WITH SOUR CREAM

Veal loin chops, or steak
Butter

½ pint sour cream
Salt and pepper

1. Brown veal, either breaded or plain, in butter.   2. Add salt and pepper and cover with sour cream and ½ pint of water.   3. Simmer, very slowly, in oven for 2 hours.

Ida Weaver.

MEAT ACCOMPANIMENTS...

APPLE RINGS

1. Wash firm apples, as Northern Spies.   2. Cut ½ inch slices crosswise, remove the core.   Cook until tender in a syrup made from: 3 parts sugar, 2 parts water, ½ cup cinnamon candies.   4. If deep color is desired, add coloring.   5. Garnish cold roast pork or ham, or use hot with hot roast.   6. Use with whipped cream for dessert.

Thera D. Wood

DUMPLINGS FOR STEW

2 cups flour
½ teaspoon salt

3 teaspoons baking powder
1 cup milk

1. Mix and sift dry ingredients.   2. Add milk and drop by spoonfuls on boiling stew.   3. Cover tightly, cook 10 minutes.

Mrs. J. C. Boody

FOWL...

BAKED CHICKEN COUNTRY STYLE

1. Cut fowl in pieces as for stewing.   2. Wash, dip each piece in flour. 3. Sprinkle with salt and pepper, dot liberally with butter.   4. Put in the oven, in a baking pan or skillet.   5. Turn each piece, as necessary, until browned.   6. Fill pan with water half way up on chicken.   7. Cover and bake slowly until very tender, turning frequently.   8. Replenish water if necessary.

Mrs. M. H. Bartley

DELICIOUS FRIED CHICKEN

1 small chicken, cut into pieces   Carrots
Potatoes   1 can consomme

1. Fry chicken until brown.   2. Remove to platter and place layer of potatoes cut ½ inch thick in bottom of the skillet.   3. Add layer of sliced carrots and another of sliced onion.   4. Place pieces of fried chicken over this and pour over all 1 can consomme.   5. Simmer slowly about 1 hour.

Mrs. J. C. Boody

OYSTER STUFFING FOR TURKEY

2 cups bread crumbs   2 eggs
2 cups oyster crackers   1 quart oysters
½ pound melted butter

1. Mix bread crumbs and crackers, with melted butter liquid from oysters and beaten eggs.   2. Add oysters and season to taste.   3. Prepare turkey as usual for stuffing and stuff lightly.

Mrs. John W. Ballard

GAME . . .

GAME DINNER

MENU

Apple Cider

Pheasant or Partridge and Woodcock

Mashed Potato   Boiled Small Onions

Fruit Salad

(pear, apple and California grapes)

Pumpkin Pie with Cheese   Coffee

Jean Sessions

PHEASANT OR PARTRIDGE

To realize the full flavor of these delicious upland game birds, they should be roasted. Either may be skinned or the feathers plucked, as with domestic fowl. While many connoisseurs believe that the birds should be hung for several days, past experience has proven that they are more delicate in flavor, if dressed and cleaned as soon after shooting, as possible. Prompt plucking is best when intact skin is desired. Birds may be kept several weeks after cleaning, by freezing in refrigerator tray.   Allow 4 hours for thawing, before preparing food for oven.

After cleaning, washing and drying, prepare stuffing as follows:
Stuffing:

3 tablespoons melted butter   Sage
2 cups bread crumbs   Cream
¼ cup raisins

1. Add chopped onion to melted butter and brown.   2. Add bread crumbs, seasoning and raisins and brown well.   3. Combine above mixture with enough cream to hold it together.

1. After stuffing birds, rub them well with salt and butter.   2. Place in covered roaster with small quantity water.   3. Roast 2½ hours — 500 F. for 15 minutes and 350 F. for remaining time. Look at birds frequently and keep small amount of water in pan at all times.

Woodcock are prepared as above and placed in roaster 45 minutes before other birds are done.

Jean Sessions

COUNTRY CLUB RABBIT

1. Cut a young rabbit in pieces for serving.   2. Sprinkle with salt and pepper, dip in flour then in egg and coat thickly with crumbs.   3. Put into a well greased baking dish and bake in hot oven, basting often with bacon fat.   4. A youn rabbit will be done in about -½- one half hour, old ones need longer using 3 tablespoons, each of bacon fat and flour, 1 teaspoon of grated onion cooking.   5. Arrange on serving dish and make a brown gravy in the pan, and 1 ½ cups stock, milk or water. (boiling). Season with ½ teaspoon salt, ¼ teaspoon paprika and 2 teaspoons tomato catsup.   6. You did remember to remove every bit of fat from the robbit, didn't you? Fat is what makes it taste strong.

Thelma Green

HASENPEFFER (RABBIT)

Cut Rabbit as for serving.   Salt & pepper,   place in deep dish in layers.   Slice medium sized onion and lay on top. Also bay leaves and fine cloves. Cover with vinegar and water using 2-3 vinegar to 1-3 water. Leave stand in this 2 days and 1 night stirring around each day.   Heat 2 tablespoons dripping or lard; do not use bacon fat or use half butter and half lard in deep frying pan with tight lid. Brown rabbit on all sides then add bay leaves and cloves and half the onion.   About ½cup liquor.   Now cover tightly and simmer slowly till tender.   Watch closely as it burns easily. Add more liquid as needed.   About the last ten minutes add 1 tablespoon seeded raisins.   Take up rabbit and make gravy by stirring one heaping tablespoon flour in cold water again adding a little of the liquor, a teaspoon of Karo syrup and salt to taste.   Do not use part water.

Mrs. Harry King

RABBIT

1. Skin rabbit, removing head and feet. Then clean.   2. Joint and soak in cold water over night.   3. Drain and place in cold water and cook until tender, about 1 hour, depending on age of rabbit.   4. Drain, dredge with flour and fry slowly in butter until brown.

Jean Sessions

VENISON DINNER

MENU

Oyster Cocktail

Consomme with Rice

Relishes   Rolls   Butter

Roast Venison with Brown Gravy   Sweet Cider

Mashed Potatoes   Brussels Sprouts   Cranberry Sauce

Head Lettuce with Fruit Dressing

Coffee

Fruit Sherbert with Assorted Cookies

Marion Mackie

ROAST VENISON

1. The shoulder, boned and rolled is very good for this roast.   2. Have salt pork rolled with the shoulder.   3. Rub the outside, of the roast with salt, pepper, and flour.   4. Brown in roaster, at 500 degrees.   5. Add several onions, 2 cloves garlic and 3 or 4 bayleaves, about ½ cup water.   6. Roast at 350º F. for about 25 minutes per pound.

Marion Mackie

VENISON CUTLETS

1. The small steaks cut from the loin are called cutlets.   2. Prepare as follows: clean and trim the cutlets.   3. Sprinkle with salt and pepper, brush over with cooking oil or melted butter.   4. Roll in dry bread crumbs, saute and serve with the following sauce.

½ cup melted butter	1 capers
1 teaspoon chopped sour pickle	3 tablespoons lemon juice
1 teaspoon chopped onion	1 egg

1. Add seasoning, chopped pickle, onion and caper to the melted butter.   2. Add lemon juice.   3. Add beaten egg yolk.   4. Last add the stiffly beaten egg white.

VENISON LIVER AND BACON

1. Slice the venison liver in ¼ inch slices.   2. Let stand 5 minutes in cold water, to draw out blood.   3. Drain and cover with boiling water to which 2 tablespoons of vinegar, to 1 quart of water, has been added.   4. Keep at boiling point, for 5 minutes.   5. Drain, sprinkle well with salt and pepper, dredge with flour and fry in bacon fat.   6. Serve with crisp bacon.   7. Putting the liver into this acidulated water, improves the flavor.

BROILED VENISON STEAK

1. Cut steak 1 ½ inches thick.   2. Wipe with a cloth wrung from cold water, being careful to remove any hairs clinging to the meat.   3. Brush the entire steak with cooking oil and place in broiler.   4. Turn every ½ minute for first 2 minutes, in order to sear the suface.   5. After the first 2 minutes, turn occasionally, until well cooked on both sides.   6. Steak cut 1 ½ inches thick, requires 10 minutes. The steak will be rare, as it should always be.   Serve with Maitre d'Hotel Butter.

VENISON STEW

The shoulder or saddle is best for stew.
1. Placethe meat in an earthen jar and cover with vinegar to which has been added 3 or 4 onions, sliced, and 6 bay leaves.   2. Allow to stnd at least 2 days before cooking.   3. Remove the meat from the brine, wash in cold water.   4. Add boiling water and stew slowly, until tender.   5. Remove meat and make gravy from the broth. Venison cooked this way is delicious, making a good dish, from undesirable cuts.

Marion Mackie

SQUIRREL

1. Skin and draw squirrel, and cut into serving pieces. Wash thoroughly and let stand in acidulated water (2 tablespoons vinegar to 1 quart of water), for 24 hours.   3. Boil in salted water, to which 3 bayleaves and 6 whole allspice have been added, about 1 hour or until tender.   4. Drain, dredge with flour, salt and pepper and fry in butter.

Marion Mackie

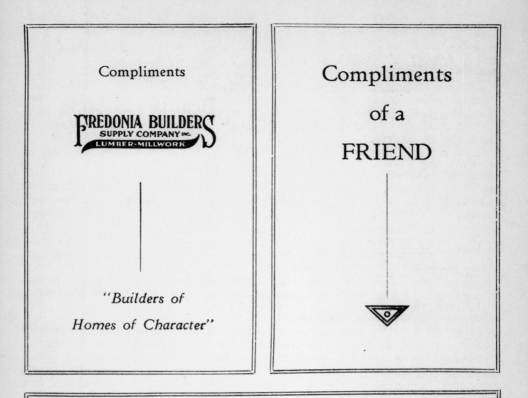

EGGS, CHEESE and CASSEROLE DISHES ...

BAKED STUFFED CAULIFLOWER

1 head cauliflower
4 slices stale bread
1 medium onion chopped
2 tablespoons butter

2 cups ground ham
½ teaspoon celery salt
1 egg
¼ cup milk

1. Wash cauliflower, leave whole and place in boiling salted water and cook two minutes. 2. Remove, drain and cool. 3. Prepare dressing by pouring cold water over bread and allowing to stand. 4. Saute onions in butter until yellow and soft, but not browned. 5. Add ground ham and stir until heated through. 6. Squeeze bread dry, add celery salt, onion, ham and beaten egg, blended with milk. Mix well. 7. Place cauliflower in greased casserole and arrange dressing where flowers have separated and pack that remaining around head. 8. Dot with butter and bake 30 minutes at 375º.

Gladys S. Quist

BOILED POT PIE

Veal Stew
1 onion
Parsley

Salt
Pepper

1. Stew veal with chopped onion, parsley and seasoning until tender. 2. Make pie of following ingredients:

3 cups flour
2 tablespoons butter
½ teaspoon salt

2 eggs
Milk enough to make a soft dough

1. Roll quite thin and cut in pieces about two by six inches. 2. Dip piece by piece in the above liquid which should be rapidly boiling. 3. Put lid on closely and cook for 20 minutes. This dish requires a generous amount of liquid on the meat before dough strips are added. It may be made with chicken instead of veal.

Edna Foss, Dunkirk

CHEESE CASSEROLE

4 slices bread spread with
2 tablespoons butter and
Teaspoon mustard
¼ teaspoon paprika
1 cup cheese

2 eggs
1½ cups milk
1 teaspoon salt
Few grains of cayenne
4 slices bacon (ground)

1. Remove crusts of bread, spread and cut in ¾ inch cubes. 2. Put in casserole. 3. Beat eggs slightly; add seasoning, cheese and bacon. 4. Pour over bread and bake 30 to 40 minutes in oven at 350º F.

Grace Smith

CHEESE CUSTARD

2 eggs
1 cup ground dry bread crumbs
1 pint milk

¾ cup grated cheese
Salt

1. Beat eggs lightly and add other ingredients. 2. Bake in buttered pudding dish in slow oven until set firm. Nice to serve with meat or fish course.

Mary Dunbar

CHEESE SOUFFLE I

3 tablespoons tapioca (minute)	1 cup milk scalded
3 egg yolks beaten thick	1 cup cheese (strong)
3 egg whites stiffly beaten with one teaspoon salt	

1. Add tapioca to milk and cook in double boiler 15 minutes, or until tapioca is clear. 2. Stir frequently. 3. Add cheese and stir until melted. 4. Cool, then add egg yolks and mix well. 5. Fold in egg whites. 6. Bake in greased dish placed in hot water in moderate oven for 50 minutes.

Norinne Walker

CHEESE SOUFFLE II

3 eggs	1 cup milk
1 cup grated cheese	2 tablespoons flour
2 tablespoons butter	Salt and pepper

1. Melt butter and stir in flour. 2. When smooth, add milk to make white sauce. 3. Add cheese, salt and pepper. 4. Beat yolks of eggs with 1 teaspoon of water until light. 5. Add to first mixture and cool. 6. Beat whites of eggs until stiff and add to cheese mixture. 7. Bake in buttered pan in slow oven 20 to 30 minutes. Serve at once.

Jenny Green

CHICKEN TIMBALES

2 cups chopped chicken	3 eggs beaten
2 tablespoons chopped parsley	1 cup milk
¾ cup soft bread crumbs	1 cup chicken stock
2 tablespoons butter	Salt and pepper

1. Mix all ingredients together and bake in ramekins set in pan of water for 45 minutes, or until set like a custard. 2. Serve with thick sauce to which mushrooms have been added.

Mrs. E. M. Bowen

CHICKEN PILAU

2 quarts chicken broth	¼ teaspoon cloves
1 cup rice	¼ teaspoon cinnamon
3 tablespoons butter	

1. Cook rice in butter slowly until it resembles pop corn — about 4 minutes. 2. Place in casserole with spices. 3. Add broth to cover 3 inches above rice. 4.. Cook covered in oven until liquid is absorbed. 5. Fry separately in butter sliced onions, peanuts and raisins. 6. Serve on top of rice on center of a platter, surrounded by fried chicken.

Dorothy Schauffler

CHILI CON CARNE I

1½ pounds lean beef ground	2 onions
3 tablespoons butter	1 green pepper, chopped
1 can tomato soup	1 cup celery, chopped
1 teaspoon chili powder	Salt and pepper
1 can red kidney beans	

1. Brown meat in butter. 2. Add remaining ingredients and cook slowly, 1 hour. Serve with plain boiled rice.

Mary E. Cook

CHILI CON CARNE II

4 tablespoon onion
4 tablespoons butter
1½ pounds ground round steak
1 pint canned tomatoes
1 can red kidney beans

1 stalk celery
2 quarts water
Salt and pepper
Chili powder to taste

1. Brown onions in butter. 2. Add ground steak and cook 5 or 10 minutes. 3. Add tomatoes, beans, cut celery, water, and seasoning. 4. Cook slowly 1 hour, stirring occasionally. 5. Thicken with flour and water.

CHILI CON CARNE NO. III

2 onions
1 quart tomatoes
2 potatoes
1 cup red kidney beans (cooked)
2 teaspoons salt

¼ teaspoon paprika
¼ teaspoon chili powder
½ teaspoon ground cloves
1 pound round steak ground
1½ tablespoons butter

1. Slice onions and cook until tender in tomatoes. 2. Cook separately the potatoes cut in small cubes in boiling, salted water. Drain. 3. Melt butter in skillet and cook ground meat, stirring frequently so that it is thoroughly cooked. 4. Combine all ingredients, mixing well. Serves six.

Frances H. Kerr

CHOP SUEY

2½ pounds veal and pork, cut finely
4 large onions
4 bunches celery
1 medium can mushrooms

2 tablespoons brown sauce (LaChoy)
4 tablespoons cornstarch
4 tablespoons soy sauce
2 cans beans sprouts

1. Fry meat until tender and brown. 2. Add mushrooms, celery and onions cut fine, and brown sauce. 3. Let simmer until celery begins to be tender. 4. When ready to serve, add sprouts, and allow to heat through throughly. 5. Make a paste of cornstarch and soy sauce and add to mixture for thickening. 6. If more liquid is needed while cooking, use that from sprouts. 7. If more seasoning is required, use soy sauce instead of salt. Serves 8 to 10 persons. May be served with LaChoy noodles or dry boiled rice.

Mildred Rogger

CREAMED SWEETBREADS

Sweetbreads
Cream sauce

Parsley
Salt and Pepper

1. Cook and skin sweetbreads. 2. Cut in cubes. 3. Make cream sauce of half milk and half cream. 4. Add seasoning and parsley and serve in patty shells or on toast.

Katherine A. Jones

CURRIED LAMB AND APPLES

1 cup chopped fried onions
1 cup diced apples
2 cups diced cooked lamb
2 cups milk

3 tablespoons butter
1 teaspoon curry powder
2 tablespoons flour

1. Place onions, apples and lamb in a casserole. 2. Cover with sauce made with milk, butter, flour and curry powder. 3. Season with salt and pepper. 4. Bake slowly 45 minutes and serve with boiled rice.

Mable S. Williams

EAST INDIAN CURRY

1 cup rice
2 to 3 quarts water
1 tablespoon lemon juice
3 onions chopped fine

1 to 3 tablespoons curry powder to taste
Small chunks of raw or cooked meat, vegetables, etc.

1. Add rice to boiling water, gradually so water does not stop boiling. 2. Add lemon juice and salt and cook until done without stirring. Drain. 3. Mix curry powder with half the amount of flour and make smooth paste with water. 4. Mince onions fine and brown in butter. 5. Combine onions, curry paste with hot water to make sauce. Season to taste with salt. 6. Add meat and vegetables and serve with rice.

Dorothy Schauffler

EGGS ON ROCKS (Out door Recipe)

1. Heat large flat stones, one to a person, for about 30 minutes in hot fire. 2. Fry a slice of bread from which all but the outside crusts have been cut, 4. Lay the crust on a stone and break egg into it. The crust prevents the egg from running off the stone.

Esther Oaks

ITALIAN RICE

2 cups cooked rice
2 cups cooked meat (hamburg)
3 tablespoons chopped onion fried in butter

2 tablespoons green pepper
1½ cups canned tomatoes or meat stock

1. Combine all ingredients and season to taste. 2. Cover with buttered crumbs and bake one hour. 3. Serve hot.

Mary Dunbar

JIFFY STEW

1 pound weiners
1 No. 2¼ can tomatoes
4 medium size potatoes

2 onions
Salt and pepper to taste

1. Slice weiners, cut potatoes in small cubes and dice onion. 2. Put in kettle with tomatoes and seasoning and simmer until potatoes are tender.

Margaret Gailewicz

KIDNEY BEAN RAREBIT

2 cups milk
4 tablespoons butter
4 tablespoons flour

½ brick cheese
1 cup canned red kidney beans
1 chopped pimento

1. Make cream sauce of first three ingredients and salt to taste. 2. Add cheese and stir until melted. 3. Add beans and pimento. 4. Serve on toast.

Mrs. H. M. Montgomery, Silver Creek

LAMB SOUFFLE

5 tablespoons butter
5 tablepsoons flour
1½ cups milk
¾ teaspoon salt
3 eggs

1 small green pepper, chopped
2 cups ground cooked lamb
2 tablespoons onion, chopped
Pepper

1. Make cream sauce of first 3 ingredients.   2. Add salt, pepper and yolks of eggs, well beaten.   3. Mix well and fold in meat.   4. Fold in stiffly beaten egg whites.   5. Pour into large or individual ring molds and place in pan of hot water.   Allow to bake in moderate oven, about 40 minutes or until it is set. 6. Serve with cream sauce.

Mrs. Robert K. Pierce

LUNCHEON GRIDDLE CAKES

1 cup steamed rice
1 cup milk
2 eggs
½ teaspoon salt

¾ cup flour
¼ cup grated cheese
1 tablespoon melted butter

1. Pour milk over warm rice   .2. Add the yolks of eggs beaten thick.   3. Add remaining ingredients.   4. Fold in stiffly beaten egg whites.   5. Drop by spoonfuls on hot griddle and cook to a delicate brown, turning as usual. Serve for luncheon with creamed mushrooms.

Jane Custer

LUNCHEON SURPRISE

2 cups flour
3 teaspoons baking powder
¾ teaspoon salt

4 tablespoons shortening
¾ cup milk
Left over meat with gravy

1. Sift dry ingredients together, mix in shortening.   2. Add milk.   3. Roll out *very* thin on well floured board.   4. Spread with chopped, well seasoned meat, which has been mixed with gravy.   5. Roll as you would a jelly roll.   6. Bake in a hot oven, 475° F. about 20 minutes.   Serve, at once, with gravy.

Jean H. Sessions

MACARONI AND CHEESE SOUFFLE

1 cup macaroni
¾ cup grated cheese
1 cup soft bread crumbs packed
½ cup melted butter
Salt and pepper

½ green pepper, chopped
1 pimento, chopped
1 ½ cups milk
3 eggs well beaten

1. Cook the macaroni in boiling water until mushy.   2. Scald the milk and pour over the above ingredients, except the eggs.   3. Beat the eggs very light and add last.   4. Set baking dish in pan of hot water.   5. Bake in moderate oven for 40 minutes.

Mrs. E. M. Bowen

MACARONI MOUSSE

1 cup elbow macaroni
1½ cups scalded milk
1 cup soft bread crumbs
¼ cup melted butter
   Small can mushrooms
3 eggs

1 pimento chopped
1 tablespoon chopped onion
1½ cups grated cheese
⅓ teaspoon salt
   Pepper
   Paprika

1. Cook macaroni, blanch in cold water and drain.   2. Pour scalding milk over bread crumbs and add butter, cheese and seasonings.   3. Add beaten eggs and bake 50 minutes in loaf pan set in water.

Mrs. C. F. Drewes, Dunkirk

NOODLES AU GRATIN

1 package noodles
1 large can condensed milk

2 cups grated cheese
1 chopped green pepper

1. Boil noodles and place in a shallow pan.   2. Boil green pepper until tender. 3. Add the pepper and milk to noodles and top with cheese.   4. Bake in slow oven until milk is absorbed.

Mrs. H. M. Montgomery, Silver Creek

NOODLE CASSEROLE

½ pound noodles
2 large onions, sliced
½ pound ground steak
1 can tomato sauce

1 medium can mushrooms
   (or ½ pound fresh)
½ medium can ripe olives sliced
½ pound cheese, cubed

1. Cook noodles in salted water and drain.   2. Fry onions in butter and add to cooked noodles.   3. Brown steak and season.   Add to noodles and onions. 4. Add remaining ingredients and mix. 5. Bake in a moderate oven (375° F.) for 45 minutes.   The mixture will seem dry and if you like things highly seasoned, you may add another half can of sauce or ¼ cup water. This may be mixed the day before it is cooked.   The receipt is a large one. Use half for a small family.

Mrs. Harold F. Smith

NOODLES, SAUERKRAUT AND SAUSAGE

1 package noodles
½ can sauerkraut

½ pound pork sausage

1. Cook and drain noodles.   2. Put half in bottom of a buttered baking dish. 3. Add layers of sauerkraut and sausage.   4. Repeat, and cook 1½ hours in moderate oven (375°).

Jane Custer

NOODLE LUNCHEON DISH (serves 20)

1 pound noodles (narrow)
1 cup bread crumbs
3 tablespoons butter
½ cup chopped pimento

¾ cup flour
1½ quarts milk
1 pound Old English cheese
1 pound dried beef

1. Cook mushrooms in butter, blend in flour, add milk and cook until thick. 2. Add broken cheese and stir until melted. 3. Add pimentos, shredded beef and noodles, cooked and drained. 4. Put in buttered casserole, cover with buttered crumbs. 5. Cook 20 to 30 minutes in moderate oven.

Mrs. Harry Peters

RICE AND MEAT BALLS

1 cup raw rice
1½ pounds hamburg
(if ground beef is used, use some fat)
1 onion, finely chopped
½ cup celery, finely chopped
Salt and pepper

1. Mix ingredients and make into small balls, 2. Cook balls very slowly for about two hours in three cups of tomato juice.

Margaret Diers

RICE AND PORK CHOPS

To serve four:
4 pork chops
1 cup cooked rice
2 medium onions
Tomato soup
Salt and pepper to taste

1. Brown and season chops. 2. Lay chops in roaster and place a medium slice of onion on each chop. 3. Place ball of cooked rice on slice of onion. 4. Pour 2 tablespoons of tomato soup over the rice on each chop. 5. Cover roaster and allow to bake slowly 1 hour. Baste frequently with remainder of tomato soup.

Katherine Regan Kane, Dunkirk

RICE PUFF

½ cup rice
3 eggs
¼ pound cheese
¾ teaspoon mustard
½ cup medium white sauce
Salt and pepper

1. Wash and cook rice. 2. Beat egg yolks and add to cooked rice and finely cut cheese. 3. Add white sauce and seasoning. 4. Fold in stiffly beaten egg whites. 5. Bake 40 minutes in 375° oven (medium).

Margaret Gailewicz

RICE SOUFFLE

1 cup uncooked rice
4 eggs
1 pint milk
¼ pound strong cheese
Salt and pepper
Paprika

1. Cook rice until nearly done. 2. Drain and rinse with cold water. 3. Make a cream sauce with milk, cheese and beaten egg yolks. 4. Add rice and fold in stiffly beaten egg whites. 5. Bake 40 minutes in 375° oven (medium).

Mrs. C. F. Drewes, Dunkirk.

SCALLOPED CHICKEN

½ cup butter
½ cup flour
1½ cups chicken stock
1 can or ½ pound fresh mushrooms
1 ½ cups milk
Salt and pepper
3 cups chicken, cut up

1. Mix all ingredients together. If fresh mushrooms are used, saute first in butter.　2. Put layer of cream mixture in buttered baking dish, then layer bread crumbs and one of chicken.　3. Repeat layers, ending with bread crumbs.　4. Bake in moderate oven until crumbs are brown. Serves about ten.

Mrs. R. I. Mulholland, Dunkirk

SIX LAYER DINNER

Arrange in layers in a casserole:　1st—Raw potatoes, 2nd—Chopped onions, 3rd—chopped celery, 4th—Round steak and pork, ground and seasoned. 5th—Canned tomatoes, 6th—Strips of bacon — after partly cooking casserole. Bake about two hours in moderate oven. Bacon may be omitted, if desired.

Gladys M. Parker

SPAGHETTI, MEAT BALLS AND SAUCE

SAUCE: (Begin by making the sauce first)

2 large cans tomatoes	¼ teaspoon nutmeg
1 small onion	¼ teaspoon cinnamon
1 can tomato paste	½ teaspoon pepper
1 tablespoon salt	½ to ¼ teaspoon soda
1 tablespoon sugar	

1. Combine the above ingredients and cook until thick, usually about 2 or 3 hours.　2. Add the sauce to the meat balls and simmer 2 or 3 hours.　3. Lastly, just before serving, pour over the spaghetti which must be kept hot.

1 package spaghetti	1 small onion, chopped
1 pound round steak ground with	½ cup cracker crumbs
	2 eggs
½ pound pork	½ wine glass of wine
1 tablespoon salt	½ cup grated cheese if desired
1 teaspoon pepper	

1. Boil the spaghetti in salted water until tender. Drain, put in a collandar and run cold water over it and drain.　2. Mix the rest of the ingredients as you would for meat loaf, form into balls.　3. Brown in butter or oil. Add the sauce to the meat balls and simmer 2 or 3 hours.

SPAGHETTI AND SAUCE

2 small bunches celery	3 cans tomato paste
5 medium onions	1 can Campbells tomato soup
1 or 2 medium cloves of garlic	1 quart water
½ to 1 green sweet pepper	3 tablespoons salt
3 tablespoon sugar	Pepper

1. Cut fine, celery, onions, garlic and sweet pepper.　2. Cook in cooking oil or Crisco 5 or 10 minutes, but do not brown.　3. Add 3 cans tomato paste, tomato soup, water, salt, sugar and pepper and cook as catsup, stirring often, usually about 2 to 3 hours.　4. Fry pork chops and 1 pound fresh mushrooms, sliced.　5. Add to sauce and cook slowly, over low fire for 1 hour.　6. Cook 2 pounds spaghetti, (left unbroken), in a large kettle of boiling salted water, for about 15 minutes or until tender but not soft.　7. Drain, dash cold water through spaghetti and drain well.　8. Serve spaghetti on plate with sauce over it and pork chop on side of plate.

Effa Matteson

SPAGHETTI WITH CHEESE

1 cup uncooked spaghetti bro- ken in pieces
½ cup soft bread crumbs
¼ cup melted butter
3 tablespoons green pepper
3 tablespoons red pepper pimento

1½ teaspoons grated onion
1½ teaspoons salt
1 cup cheese
1½ cups milk, scalded
3 egg yolks
2 egg whites beaten separately

1. Combine all ingredients in order given except the spaghetti and egg whites. melted. 3. Add ice and the olives sliced. 4. Bake in casserole topped with but-greased pan for 45 minutes. Serves six.

Norinne Walker

SPANISH CASSEROLE

2 cups milk
4 tablespoons butter
4 tablespoons flour
Salt and pepper

½ brick Chateau cheese
½ cup stuffed olives
1 ½ cups boiled rice

1. Make cream sauce of first four ingredients. 2. Add cheese and stir until melted. 3. Add ice and the olives sliced. 4. Bake in casserole topped with but-tered crumbs.

Mrs. H. M. Montgomery, Silver Creek

STUFFED CABBAGE MEAT

1 large head of cabbage
1 ½ pounds of hamburg
1 can tomatoes
1 lemon

¾ cup brown sugar
2 eggs
1 onion, browned
Salt and pepper

1. Select a large, leafy cabbage, cut core at center and loosen the leaves. 2. Pour boiling water over cabbage, cover and let steam 5 minutes, drain off water and dry leaves. 3. One cup bread crumbs combined with eggs, minced onion, hamburg and seasoning. 4. Brown a little of onion in butter in a kettle in which cabbage is to be cooked. 5. Make small rolls of meat mix-ture and wrap in a cabbage leaf. 6. Place rolls in kettle and add canned tomatoes, lemon juice, brown sugar and salt to taste. 7. Boil until juice thickens, then brown in oven.

Mrs. Harry Ballotin

VEGETABLE CASSEROLE

3 pounds beef
3 medium sized onions
6 carrots, diced or sliced
6 meium potatoes
¼ cup flour

3 stalks celery
2 cups green beans (fresh or canned)
2 cups corn, (fresh or canned)
Water to almost cover

1. Cut beef into small pieces, for stewing. 2. Dredge with flour, salt and pepper to taste and brown in melted fat with onion. 3. Place meat and vegetables, alternately in large roasting pan, covered, 4. Bake in slow oven, at least 3 hours. If a thicker gravy is desired, add more water and flour.

Esther Rabin

WELSH RAREBIT

1 large tablespoon butter	½ pound sharp cheese, grated
2 teaspoons cornstarch	½ teaspoons salt
½ teaspoon dry mustard	Pepper
2 cups top milk	

1. Cook butter, cornstarch, mustard and milk in double boiler until thick. 2. Add grated cheese, salt and pepper. 3. Cook until cheese is melted. Serve hot on toast or crackers.

Mrs. M. B. Douthett, Pittsburgh

VEGETABLES . . .

ASPARAGUS WITH BUTTER SAUCE

Cook the asparagus in boiling salted water as usual. When tender, serve with the following sauce:

½ cup butter	¼ teaspoon salt
2 egg yolks	Dash of cayenne
1 tablespoon lemon juice	½ cup boiling water or milk

1. Mix the egg yolks and lemon juice and 1-3 of the butter. 2 Cook and keep stirring. While stirring add the remainder of the butter - 1 tablespoon at a time — seasoning and water or milk. If the mixture curdles, add a little cream. Serves 6.

Dora Douglas.

BROCCOLI WITH MOCK HOLLANDAISE SAUCE

Soak the broccoli in cold salted water to draw out the insects. Cut off the withered leaves, split the heavy stalks in two. Cook in boiling salted water as you would for asparagus and serve with the following sauce:

Mock Hollandaise Sauce

2 egg yolks	2 ½ tablespoons lemon juice
1 cup thick white sauce	Few grains cayenne

1. Beat the egg yolks, add to the hot white sauce and mix well. Cook 2 minutes, stirring constantly. Remove from fire, add lemon juice and cayenne. Pour over the broccoli and serve hot.

Lois M. Thompson.

CORN OYSTERS

1 dozen ears corn	2 teaspoons sugar
Salt	4 eggs
Pepper	

1. Cut the corn off the ear. 2. Add salt, sugar, pepper and egg yolks. 3. Beat egg whites stiffly and fold into mixture. 4. Drop from spoon to make small oyster-sized portions and fry in hot lard on both sides. Serve piping hot.

Edna Foss.

COOKED CABBAGE WITH SAUCE

1 medium sized cabbage	Salt and pepper
¼ cup vinegar	¼ cup hot water
2 tablespoons sugar	½ tablespoon mustard
1 tablespoon flour	2 tablespoons butter

1. Chop cabbage and cook until tender. Drain. 2. Mix sauce ingredients well and pour over the cabbage.

Mrs. M. H. Anderson.

CREAMED BEANS

1 quart string beans	1 teaspoon grated cheese
2 tablespoons butter	Pinch allspice
1 cup milk or cream	1 tablespoon lemon juice
1 egg	

Either fresh or canned string beans may be used for this.   If fresh beans are used, cook as usual in boiling salted water until done.   If canned beans are used, heat thoroughly.   Drain and add 2 tablespoons butter.   Combine the milk, egg, cheese and allspice.   Add the lemon juice and allow sauce to simmer for 15 minutes.   Pour over the beans and serve very hot.

Norinne Walker.

GERMAN RED CABBAGE

1 small head red cabbage	1 teaspoon salt
3 tablespoons butter	1 teaspoon sugar
1 onion	2 tablespoon vinegar
½ cup water	1 apple

1. Melt the butter in a large sauce pan.   2. Add the chopped onion, cook slightly. 3. Add finely shredded cabbage.   Fry only a short time.   4. Add water, salt sugar, vinegar.   Simmer slowly 1 1-2 hours.   5. Add chopped apple and cook ½ hour longer.

Mrs. E. W. Christoffers.

SATURDAY NIGHT BEANS

1 can baked beans	½ teaspoon Worcestershire sauce
2 strips bacon	¼ teaspoon mustard

1. Cut bacon into small bits and fry until crisp.   2. Add beans to skillet, stir in Worcestershire sauce and mustard.   Salt to taste.   3. Stir thoroughly and and serve hot.

Louise S. Butler.

SMOTHERED   LETTUCE

4 bunches leaf lettuce	1 teaspoon salt
½ cup spring onions, cut fine	1 tablespoon sugar
⅓ cup chopped bacon	¼ cup diluted vinegar

1. Mix lettuce and onions and place in a covered pan over a low flame until slightly wilted.   2. Fry the bacon slowly until crisp.   3. Add the seasoning to the vinegar and heat.   Pour over the greens, add the bacon and toss lightly with a fork until well mixed.   Serve while hot.

Lois M. Thompson

SOUTHERN   CORN   PUDDING

3 eggs beaten separately	1 tablespoon sugar
2 cups corn (canned or green)	1 tablesopon melted butter
1½ cups milk	⅛ teaspoon soda added to milk
½ teaspoon salt	

1. Add milk, salt, sugar and soda to the beaten egg yolks.   2. Add corn to the liquid.   Stir in the melter butter.   3. Add the beaten egg whites.   4. Bake in greased baking dish in moderate oven 45 minutes.   Cover   for the first 30 minutes

Mrs. Daniel Harmon

STUFFED CABBAGE

1 medium-sized head cabbage	1 teaspoon salt
1 onion	Pepper
2 strips bacon	3 tablespoons ketchup
1 pound chopped, uncooked lamb	¼ teaspoon Worcestershire sauce

1. Cook cabbage head 30 minutes. Drain and cool. Cut out the center. 2. Mince onion and cook with diced bacon until light brown. 3. Add the lamb and cook 5 minutes. 4, Add the remaining ingredients and mix well. 5. Fill the cabbage with the mixture and bake in a covered casserole in moderate oven (350○) for 35 minutes.   6. Garnish with crisp bacon.

Gladys Parker

STUFFED EGGPLANT

1 medium eggplant	Salt
1 cup grated cheese	Pepper
3 fresh tomatoes or 1 cup canned tomatoes slightly drained	1 medium onion, grated

1. Cut eggplant lengthwise and scoop out the center.   Parboil the center part until tender. Drain and combine with the cheese, tomatoes and seasoning. 3. Pack into the shells and sprinkle crumbs on top and dot with butter.   4. Bake slowly 30-45 minutes at 350○.

Elizabeth Wolfe

SWEET BAKED BEANS

2 pounds beans	1 cup sugar
1 pound salt pork	1 cup maple syrup
1 teaspoon mustard	½ teaspoon salt
1 large onion	

1. Soak the beans overnight. Drain. 2. Place all ingredients in pan and bake slowly for 6 to 8 hours.

Mildred Rogger

SWEET POTATOES A LA CASSEROLE

5 large large sweet potatoes	2 tablespoons water
1 cup brown sugar	¼ pound butter.
4 large cooking apples	Salt

1. Pare potatoes and cut in small pieces. Cook until partly done.   2. Place in layers in caasserole with sliced and pared apples, butter, sugar, salt and water.   3. Bake in moderate oven, 1 hour.

Lotta L. Dean

TAMALE RING

2 cups crushed canned corn	1 teaspoon salt
1 cup yellow corn meal	1 can tomato paste
1 small onion, chopped fine	2 eggs, beaten
½ or less green pepper., chopped fine	1 cup milk
2 tablespoons melted butter	¼ teaspoon pepper

1. Mix ingredients in order given.   2. Pour into well-greased mold (8-inch) about 2 inches deep.   3. Set mold in pan of hot water and bake slowly for one hour.   4. Serve with creamed chicken, tuna fish, mushrooms or other desired creamed mixture.

Dorothy Sievert

WESTMINSTER CABBAGE

1 medium head cabbage	¼ cup vinegar
4 tablespoons butter	1 cup boiling water
1 onion	4 tablespoons sugar
1 large apple	

1. Cook vinegar, sugar and water together for ten minutes.   2. Shred cabbage finely.   3. Cover with boiling water and let stand for five minutes. Drain.   4. Fry diced onion in butter until lightly browned, then add apple which has been sliced but not peeled.   5. Combine all ingredients.   Mix lightly and cook uncovered for about 15 minutes.   Serve immediately.

Lois Thompson

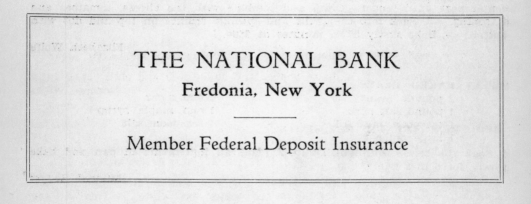

SALAD DRESSINGS . . .

FRENCH DRESSING

½ cup sugar
1 teaspoon salt
1 teaspoon mustard

1½ teaspoons paprika
½ cup vinegar
1 cup oil

1. Beat together first four ingredients. Add vinegar and oil alternately.

Clara Wheelock

FRUIT SALAD DRESSING

8 egg yolks
1 cup sugar
1 teaspoon mustard

½ teaspoon salt
2 tablepoons flour
2 cups pineapple juice

1. Beat the egg yolks, add sugar, mustard, salt and flour. Combine with the pineapple juice. 3. Cook in double boiler until thick.

Mrs. Fred Bullock

MINERAL OIL DRESSING

1 cup mineral oil
⅓ cup lemon juice
¼ cup catsup
Garlic clove or onion to taste

1 tablespoon Worcestershire sauce
¼ teaspoon salt
2 tablespoons brown sugar

1. Put all ingredients in a jar or shaker and shake well and chill before using.

Norinne Walker

REDUCER'S FRENCH DRESSING

2 eggs
½ teaspoon salt

3 tablespoons lemon juice
1¼ cups American oil

1. Add salt to egg yolks and beat hard. 2. Add lemon juice, then add oil— 1 tablespoon at a time. 3. Fold in the beaten egg whites. This will keep indefinitely.

Marguerite Taft

RED FRENCH DRESSING

1 teaspoon dry mustard
1 teaspoon salt
¼ teaspoon pepper
2 tablespoons sugar
1 teaspoon paprika
1 medium onion, minced or juice

1 tablespoon Worcestershire sauce
1½ cups olive oil
¾ cup vinegar
1 can Campbell's tomato soup

Mix all ingredients together in a quart jar and shake well. This will keep indefinitely if kept in the ice box.

Effa Matteson

RUSSIAN DRESSING

1 cup sugar
1 cup water
Juice of 2 lemons
2 tablespoons Worcestershire
sauce
1 teaspoon paprika

1 cup catsup
2 cups oil
1 tablespoon celery salt
1 teaspoon salt
2 tablespoons grated onion

1. Boil sugar, water and lemon juice together. 2. Cool. 3. Add remaining ingredients. Vinegar may be used for one-half the lemon juice. This recipe makes one quart of dressing which will keep indefinitely.

Norinne Walker

SALAD DRESSING

6 tablespoons sugar
½ teaspoon mustard
¼ teaspoon salt
1 tablespoon cornstarch mixed
with a little water

4 eggs
1 cup vinegar
½ cup water
1 tablespoon melted butter

1. Mix the dry ingredients, except the cornstarch, and add to eggs which have been beaten in the top of the double boiler. 2. Add vinegar and water slowly.. 3. Add the moistened cornstarch. 4. Stir constantly, until dressing is thick and smooth. 5.Cool and store in covered jar in refrigerator until needed.

Mrs. Fred Bullock

SWEET SALAD DRESSING

½ cup sugar
2 tablepoons flour
1 egg
Juice of 1 lemon

1 cup pineapple juice
½ pint whipping cream
Salt

1. Mix flour and sugar. 2. Add egg and mix well. 3. Add the lemon juice and pineapple juice. 4. Cook in double boiler until thick. 5. Let stand until cold. 6. Whip cream and fold into the mixture.

Elsie Pierce

SALADS . . .

AVOCADO PEAR SALAD

1 can tuna fish	California grapes
1 apple	Mayonnaise

1. Cut Avocado pears the long way. 2. Remove pit by cutting around in circle and scooping. 3. Mix apple and grapes with tuna fish. 4. Add mayonnaise. 5. Stuff one-half pear with mixture. 6. Garnish with stuffed olive and dash of paprika.

Ida Weaver

CHEESE SALAD

Juice 1 lemon	1 tablespoon gelatine
1 cup sugar	½ pint cream, whipped
1 pint pineapple juice	1 cup grated yellow cheese

1. Cook sugar, lemon juice and pineapple juice for five minutes. 2. Add gelatine softened in water, stirring until dissolved. Cool. 3. Add whipped cream and cheese. 4. Mold. Serve with mayonnaise dressing with celery, onion and green pepper cut into it.

Elizabeth Allan, Lockport, N. Y.

CHEESE AND TOMATO SALAD

1 ½ packages cream cheese	3 teaspoons lemon juice
¼ cup chopped green pepper	Dash paprika
¼ cup chopped almonds	¼ cup cream whipped
⅛ teaspoon salt	

1. Cream cheese until soft. 2. Add other ingredients. 3. Add stiffly beaten cream. 4. Pack in refrigerator tray about three-quarter inch thick. 5. Leave in freezing compartment until firm. 6. Cut into small squares and serve on slices of tomato arranged on lettuce. 7. Serve with mayonnaise.

Margaret Gregory

CHEF SALAD

1 clove garlic	2 large heads lettuce
2 hard boiled eggs	French dressing (recipe below)
1 large green pepper	
1 large onion	6 slices Swiss cheese
1 bunch celery	

1. Chop garlic very fine. 2. Add eggs, pepper and onion and chop coarsely. 3. Add celery cut up. 4. Cut up lettuce in coarse pieces. 5. Mix all ingredients in large pan. 6. Salt to taste. 7. Add dressing and mix thoroughly. 8. Add Swiss cheese cut up.

Chef Salad Dressing

1 tablespoon sugar	Oil
¼ teaspoon salt	Vinegar
¼ teaspoon paprika	

1. Into a one-half pint jar put dry ingredients. 2. Fill jar one-third full of vinegar and two-thirds full of oil. 3. Shake well just before using. This recipe serves 8 generously.

Ethel S. Graf

COTTAGE CHEESE SALAD

1 pint cottage cheese
1 cup chopped celery
½ cup chopped cucumber

1 cup chopped green pepper
1 small onion, chopped fine
3 tablespoons mayonnaise

1. Mix well and season highly with salt, paprika and cayenne pepper. 2. Dissolve one package gelatine in 1-4 cup cold water and place cup in hot water until gelatine becomes liquid. 3. Stir into cheese mixture. 4. Mold in a ring and serve on lettuce with tomatoes cut in quarters and cup of mayonnaise in center.

Mrs. Daniel A. Reed (From the Congressional Cookbook)

CRANBERRY SALAD

1 package lemon Jello
1½ cups boiling water
Juice and rind of 1 orange
or enough to make ½ cup

2 cups ground cranberries
½ cup nut meats

1. Dissolve lemon Jello in hot water. 2. Add rind and one-half cup orange juice. 3. Let Jello mixture cool. 4. Add cranberries and nuts. 5. Put in molds and chill. 6. Serve on lettuce with mayonnaise.

Elsie Pierce

FRESH GREEN SALAD

8 one-inch croutons
1 head endive
1 head lettuce
1 cucumber, sliced
1 heart celery

4 spring onions
4 tomatoes cut in eighths
¼ pound cheese cut in narrow
strips

1. Marinate croutons in French dressing. 2. Cut up all vegetables 3. Add marinated croutons and cheese strips. 4. When ready to serve add Red Dressing. 5. Mix carefully with fork.

Mrs. Harry Melin

FROZEN FRUIT SALAD—I

1 can fruit salad
½ cup cherries
2 bananas sliced
1 teaspoon gelatine

1 tablespoon cold water
1 cup mayonnaise
½ pint cream whipped

1. Drain fruit. 2. Add cherries and bananas. 3. Add gelatine dissolved in water. 4. Add mayonaise. 5. Fold in whipped cream. 6. Freeze in refrigerator tray without stirring. 7. Serve on lettuce.

Margaret Gregory

FROZEN FRUIT SALAD—II

4 cakes Philadelphia Cream
Cheese (¾ lb.)
1 small can sliced pineapple
1 medium can white cherries

1 cup mayonnaise
1 teaspoon gelatine
½ cup chopped almonds or
English walnuts

1. Cream cheese with juice of pineapple until it is of whip[...]
tency. 2. Add diced pineapple and pitted cherries, mayo[...]
3. Add gelatine dissolved in cold water. 4. Freeze in el[...]
about four hours.

FROZEN VEGETABLE SALAD

6 large tomatoes
1 cucumber
1 green pepper, cut fine
1 stalk celery, cut fine
1 tablespoon grated onion

½ teaspoon grated horseradish
¾ teaspoon salt
2 cups mayonnaise
1 cup cream, whipped

1. Peel and cube tomatoes and peel and slice cucumber thinly. 2. Mix whipped cream with salad dressing. 3. Combine all above ingredients and half the dressing and cream mixture. (Reserve other half to pour over salad when serving). 4. Freeze in electric refrigerator. Serves 8.

Frances H. Kerr

GELATINE SALAD

2 tablespoons gelatine
4 tablespoons cold water
1 cup hot water
3 tablespoons vinegar
1 tablespoon sugar
½ teaspoon salt
1 cup tuna fish

3 tablespoons relish or 3 sweet
  pickles
2 teaspoons pimentos
3 stalks celery
3 hard boiled eggs, chopped
½ cup cream, whipped
½ cup tart salad dressing

1. Soak gelatin in cold water. 2. Mix it with hot water, vinegar, sugar, salt. 3. Let cool and become partly set. 4. Mix in other ingredients. 5. Chill and serve on lettuce.

Mrs. William E. Barth

GERMAN POTATO SALAD—I

8 large potatoes
1 onion
¼ pound bacon
2 tablespoons sugar
1 teaspoon salt

1 tablespoon flour
Black pepper
¼ cup vinegar
¾ cup water
½ cup sour or sweet cream

1. Boil potatoes with skins on. 2. Cool, peel and slice. 3. Add onion sliced.

Dressing

1. Fry bacon cut up in small pieces. 2. Remove pieces of bacon. 3. Add flour to drippings. 4. Add water, vinegar and seasoning. 5. Cook until thick. 6. Add cream last. 7. Pour over potatoes hot. 8. Garnish with lettuce and crisp bacon.

Mrs. Raymond W. Foley

GERMAN POTATO SALAD—II

12 medium sized potatoes
1 small stalk celery, cut fine
1 onion, cut fine
1 tablespoon chopped parsley
3 hard cooked eggs, sliced

½ cup vinegar diluted with ½
  cup cold water
½ teaspoon dry mustard
Salt and pepper
4 slices bacon, cut fine and
  browned

. Boil potatoes in their jackets until tender. 2. Peel and dice and add the celery, hard boiled eggs, vinegar and water. 3. Add to bacon and fat, blend carefully. May be served hot or cold.

Esther Rabin

GINGER ALE SALAD

2 packages lemon Jello
2 cups ginger ale
1 cup fruit juice
1 cup grapefruit cut in small pieces

1 cup oranges, cut in small pieces
1 cup broken walnut meats
½ cup celery cut very fine

1. Dissolve the Jello in 1 cup of boiling water. 2. Add the 2 cups of ginger ale and 1 cup of fruit juice. 3. Let the fruit drain and when the jello begins to thicken, add the rest of the ingredients. Pour into a wet mold and chill. Serves 12.

Dora Douglass

GINGER PINEAPPLE SALAD

2 packages cream cheese
2 tablespoons ginger syrup
½ cup candied ginger chopped
1 cup cream whipped

1 tablespoon gelatine
2 tablespoons cold water
2 tablespoons hot water
Pineapple slices

1. Soften cream cheese with ginger syrup. 2. Add ginger, cream and gelatine that has been softened in cold water and dissolved in hot water. 3. Turn into individual molds. 4. Chill. 5. Serve on pineapple slices arranged on lettuce leaves. 6. Serve with cream mayonnaise.

Jane Custer

GREEN PEPPER SALAD

3 medium sized green peppers
½ lb. grated American cheese
Salt

½ cup chopped nuts
½ cup chopped stuffed olives
Mayonnaise

1. Remove tops from peppers. 2. Scoop out seeds and chill. 3. Mix cheese, nuts, olives and moisten with mayonnaise as needed. 4. Season with salt and paprika to taste. 5. Pack in green peppers and chill well. 6. Slice and serve on lettuce with mayonnaise. Also nice as garnish.

Alice Lane

HAM SALAD

2 cups cooked rice
1 cup diced ham

1 cup diced celery
1 small green pepper, chopped

1. Combine the above ingredients. 2. Moisten with mayonnaise.

Emma L. Hart

PEAR AND GRAPE SALAD

1 can pears
1 package cream cheese

Green grapes
Dates

1. Arrange pear halves on lettuce. 2. Fill centers with cheese. 3. Garnish with grapes and strips of dates. 4. Serve with French Dressing.

Katherine A. Jones

PINEAPPLE SALAD

1 pint grated pineapple
¾ cup sugar
Pinch of salt
½ cup cold water

1 tablespoon Knox's gelatine
2 packages cream cheese
1 pint heavy cream

1. Add the sugar and salt to the pineapple and cook five minutes.   2. Soak the gelatine in the cold water while the above is cooking.   3. Add to the mixture while still warm and beat in the cream cheese and beat some more. 4. When cool, add the cream which has been whipped.   Very nice in molds. Serves 16 people.

Clara B. Sessions

POPCORN SALAD

2 eating apples
French dressing
1 dozen white grapes, seeded

6 prunes, cooked and sliced
1 cup freshly popped corn

1. Pare and dice apples.   2. Cover with French dressing.   3. Add grapes and prunes.   4. Let stand until serving time.   5. Fold in 1 cup corn freshly popped.   6. Garnish salad bowl with lettuce.

Jane Custer

RECEPTION SALAD

Juice from 1 large can
crushed pineapple
1 package lemon Jello
Crushed pineapple from can
2 packages cream cheese

1 small can pimentos
½ cup celery cut fine
⅔ cup walnut meats cut fine
½ pint cream whipped
½ teaspoon salt

1. Boil pineapple juice.   2. Mix with jello.   3. Let stand until it begins to set. 4. Add other ingredients in order given.   5.Pour into molds. 6. Chill in refrigerator.

Mrs. H. A. King

ROSY CINNAMON APPLE SALAD

1 cup cinnamon drops
2 ½ cups boiling water
8 medium baking apples

¾ cup sugar
1 package cream cheese
¼ cup chopped nuts

1. Core and pare apples.   2. Dissolve the cinnamon drops in the boiling water and drop in the apples.   3. Cook very slowly and turn frequently.   4. When apples are done remove to a shallow dish.   5. Add the sugar to the cinnamon syrup and boil until it thickens. 6. Pour over the apples, turning them carefully in order to glaze each.   7. Cool.   Stuff with cream cheese, which has been moistened with mayonnaise, and nuts.   Serve on lettuce.

Lois M. Thompson

TOMATO JELLY SALAD

1 package strawberry Jello
2 cups boiling tomato juice

1 teaspoon salt
2 teaspoon horseradish

1. Add boiling tomato juice to Jello.   2. Season with salt and horseradish. 3. Place in molds to chill.   4. Serve on lettuce and garnish with mayonnaise.

Ida Weaver

TUNA MOLDED SALAD

½ envelope Knox gelatine
¼ cup cold water
1 cup tuna fish
2 tablespoons olives, chopped
½ cup celery

½ green pepper, chopped
¾ cup salad dressing
1 teaspoon vinegar
Salt, paprika

1. Soak gelatine in cold water 5 minutes. Add this to the salad dressing which has been heated in double boiler. 2. Cool and add the remaining ingredients. Makes 6 molds.

Jeannette Tuohy

TWENTY-FOUR HOUR FRUIT SALAD

2 eggs
4 tablespoons vinegar
4 tablespoons sugar
2 tablespoons butter
1 cup whipping cream
2 cup seeded grapes cut in half
2 cups diced pineapple

2 large oranges cut in pieces
2 cups marshmallows quartered
1 tablespoon plain gelatine
1 small bottle maraschino
cherries
½ cup salted almonds

1. Beat eggs and place in top of double boiler. 2. Add sugar, vinegar and gelatine soaked in water. 3. Beat until mixture is thick and smooth. 4. Remove from fire and add the butter. 5. Let cool. 6. When cold fold in whipped cream, fruit and marshmallows. 7. Turn into fancy mold and place on ice for 24 hours and then unmold on lettuce and sprinkle with salted nuts.

Alice Lane

VEGETABLE SALAD

3 medium-sized carrots
½ cup peanuts

½ cup raisins
Mayonnaise

1. Grind carrots, peanuts, 2. Add raisins and mayonnaise to make mixture stick together. Serve on lettuce.

Dorothy Schauffler

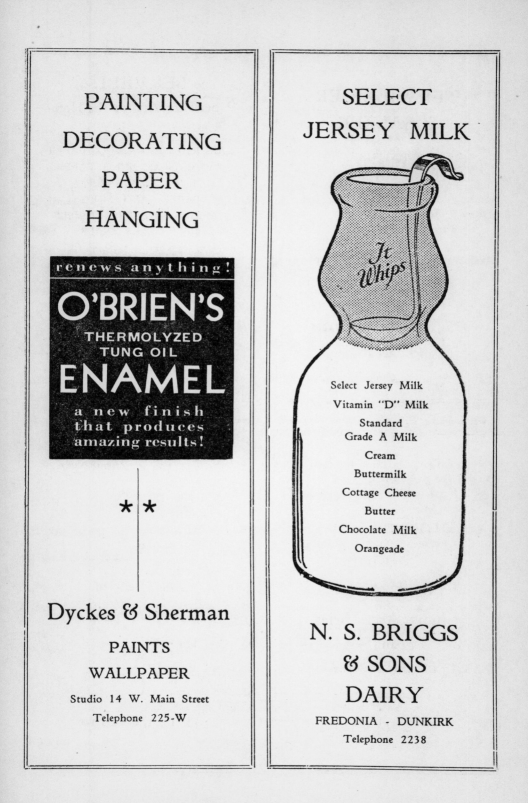

BREADS...

BREADS MADE WITH YEAST...

BREAD

1 pint milk, scalded
2 tablespoons shortening —
Crisco and butter
2 tablespoons sugar

1 teaspoon salt
1 Fleishman's yeast cake
Flour

1. Put the sugar, shortening and salt into a large mixing bowl and pour over them the scalded milk. Let stand until lukewarm. 2. In the meantime, dissolve the yeast in one-half cup of warm water and when liquid is sufficiently cool, add the yeast to it. 3. Stir in enough flour to beat well 200 times, then add enough flour to mix into a stiff loaf. 4. Turn out on a floured board and knead lightly until dough is smooth and elastic to touch and will not stick to board or hands. 5. Put dough into well greased bowl, brush the top with melted fat and set in warm place. Let rise to 3 times its bulk. 6. Shape into loaves and place in oiled pans. Let rise to double its bulk. 7. Bake in moderately hot oven (350°) 50 - 60 minutes.

Jessie Hillman

OATMEAL BREAD

3 cups uncooked Mother's
quick oatmeal
1 tablespoon salt
½ cup molasses—fill cup with
water to make 1 cup

2 tablespoons shortening
1 quart hot water
1 yeast cake, dissolved in ½
cup warm water
8 cups flour or more

1. Put the oatmeal, salt, molasses with the water and the shortening in a bowl and pour over this the quart of hot water. Let stand until cool. 2. Add the dissolved yeast cake and beat in the flour a little at a time. Make into a stiff loaf. Do this at night and let stand until morning.. 3. In the morning knead this down, shape into loaves, put in greased bread pans and let rise until light. Bake in a moderate oven.

Evelyn C. Fairbanks

WHOLE WHEAT BREAD

1 cake compressed yeast, soaked ½ hour in warm water
with
1 tablespoon sugar
1 quart tepid water and milk
3 heaping teaspoons salt

4 tablespoons shortening
¼ cup sugar
10 cups whole wheat flour
2 cups white flour
1 cup raisins dredged with
flour

1. Sift dry ingredients into bowl while dissolving yeast. 2. Place all ingredients in bowl and let rise. 3. Knead and make into 3 loaves. 4. Let rise to twice their bulk. 5. Bake in moderate oven (350°) about an hour.

Thera D. Wood

ROLLS...

DELICIOUS ROLLS

2 cakes yeast
1 tablespoon sugar
1 cup scalded milk
½ cup shortening

3 eggs
1 teaspoon salt
½ cup sugar
4½ - 5 cups flour

1. Dissolve yeast in sugar and 2 tablespoons cold water and allow to stand while mixing dough.　2. Scald milk, add shortening, sugar, eggs and salt. Beat thoroughly.　3. Add 2 cups flour, dissolved yeast and balance of the flour. Allow to rise to double its bulk.　4. Form into any shaped rolls and let rise. 5. Bake in a hot oven.

This recipe may be varied by putting brown sugar, butter and nuts into the baking pan and placing the rolls on top of this and then let rise; or roll dough out and sprinkle with cinnamon, butter and sugar. Roll up and slice off in inch or 1 1-2 inch slices and place in pan with the cut side up.

Mrs. Robert Gardner

CORN MEAL ROLLS

¾ cup corn meal boiled in
1 pint milk until mush is
  formed
⅔ cup lard
2 yeast cakes

½ cup water
⅓ cup sugar
1 teaspoon salt
2 beaten eggs
4½ cups flour

1. Add lard to mush and let cool. 2. Dissolve yeast cake in ½ cup water and add.　3. Sift flour, sugar and salt together and combine.　4. Add the well-beaten egg.　4. Make into a loaf and let rise 2 hours. (An additional 1-2 cup of flour will be needed in kneading the dough on the board.) Let rise 2 hours.　Bake in a hot oven.

Clara Wheelock

FINGER ROLLS

1 cup milk
½ cup lard
½ cup sugar
1 yeast cake

2 beaten eggs
4½ cups flour
½ teaspoon salt

1. Scald milk and add the sugar and lard.　2. Dissolve yeast in 1 tablespoon cold water.　3. When milk has cooled, add other ingredients.　4. Let rise to double its bulk, then divide in half.　4. Roll out like a pie crust. Cut in quarters, then cut each piece in 4 pieces.　5. Roll from large end and place on tin leaving plenty of space. 6. Let rise until very light.　Bake 8 minutes in a hot oven.

Mildred Rogger

POLLY'S ICE BOX ROLLS

2 yeast cakes
1 cup boiling water
1 cup Crisco
2 eggs

5 tablespoons sugar
2 teaspoons salt
6 cups sifted flour
½ cup water

1. Dissolve yeast cakes in a little warm water.　2. Pour boiling water over the Crisco. Combine the two when cool.　3. Beat the eggs and add the sugar and salt. Combine with the first mixture. 5. Sift the flour and beat in.　6. Add enough water (½ cup) to make a soft dough.　7. Let stand in icebox 2 hours. 8. Make into rolls and let stand 2 hours. Bake in a moderate oven.　Makes 4 dozen clover leaf rolls or 6 dozen small rolls. This dough will last a week if kept well covered.

Cora Sawyer Scott.

REFRIGERATOR ROLLS

1 cup butter
½ cup sugar
1 tablespoon salt
1 cup boiling water

2 yeast cakes, softened in
1 cup lukewarm water
2 eggs, beaten
6 cups unsifted flour

1. Mix butter (or other shortening), sugar, salt and boiling water together.
2. When cooled to lukewarm, add softened yeast. Add eggs and mix well.
3. Sift flour slowly into the mixture and beat hard.   4. Cover and place in refrigerator until chilled. 5. Shape into rolls and let rise in warm place 2 hours.
6. Bake in a hot oven (400o F.) for 20 minutes.

Mrs. Harold Smith

COFEEE CAKES WITH YEAST . . .

COFFEE CAKE

2 cups scalded milk
1 cup sugar
1 tablespoon butter
1 tablespoon lard

1 tablespoon salt
2 yeast cakes
6½ cups flour

1. Scald the milk and add the shortening, sugar and salt.   2. Dissolve the yeast
in a little lukewarm water. When milk mixture is cool, add the yeast.   3. Stir
in the flour gradually and beat well. 4. Let rise until double in bulk. 5.Knead
down and put in two buttered tins. Let rise again, cover the top with melted
sugar and melted butter.   Bake 30 minutes in oven 375o - 400o.

Mrs. R. I. Mulholland.

GERMAN CINNAMON OR COFFEE CAKE

2 cups lukewarm milk
1 tablespoon butter
1 tablespoon lard
2 cakes yeast

1 cup sugar
2 well-beaten eggs
6 cups flour
1 teaspoon salt

1. Dissolve butter and lard in 1 cup milk.   2. Dissolve yeast cakes in other.
3. Stir sugar and eggs until blended.   4. Add liquid, flour and salt.   5. Let
rise until double in quantity, then put in pans — one 8x12 inch or 2 square pans.
Let rise again until very light.   6. Cover top with mixture of cinnamon, brown
sugar and melted butter.   Bake 30 minutes in oven 375o - 400o.

Elizabeth G. Woodin.

BAKING POWDER BREADS . . .

BANANA NUT BREAD

2 cups flour
1 teaspoon baking powder
1 teaspoon soda
1 teaspoon salt
2 eggs

1 tablespoon water
1 cup white sugar
½ cup lard
½ cup nut meats

1. Sift all dry ingredients.   2. Mash bananas.   3. Add sugar and water, let
stand 15 minutes.   4. Cream lard and add banana mixture. Beat. 5. Add
dry ingredients.   6. Add beaten eggs, nuts.   7. Bake 50-60 minutes in moderate
oven.

Abbie Walker

BROWN BREAD

1 cup white sugar
1 cup brown sugar
4 cups rich sour cream
4 teaspoons soda

2 cups white flour
4 cups graham flour
½ teaspoon salt

1. Sift dry ingredients and mix well with cream.   2. Make into 2 good-sized loaves.   3. Bake in moderate oven about 1 hour.

Marguerite Taft.

DATE BREAD I

1½ cups sugar
2 eggs
3 tablespoon melted lard
1 teaspoon vanilla
Salt

3 cups flour
1 cup dates
2 cups boiling water
2 teaspoons soda

1. Stone dates and cut into small pieces.   2. Sprinkle soda over dates.   3. Cover with boiling water.   4. When cool, add other ingredients.   5. Bake slowly.

Clara Wheelock

DATE BREAD II

1 cup dates
½ cup walnuts
1 teaspoon soda
1 cup boiling water
½ cup white sugar

1 heaping teaspoon butter
1 egg
1½ cups flour
Salt

1. Cut dates and nuts.   2. Add soda and water.   Mix remaining ingredients and add.   4. Bake slowly for 1 hour and 10 minutes.

Alice Monroe

GRAHAM BREAD I

½ cup sugar
2 tablespoons lard
1 egg
½ teaspoon salt

2 cups sour milk
2 level teaspoons soda
1 cup white flour
2 cup graham flour

1. Cream lard, add sugar, egg, salt.   2. Add soda to sour milk and add to first mixture.   3. Beat in white flour, then graham flour.   4. Bake in greased bread tin 45 minutes in a 350° oven.

Mrs. Robert K. Pierce

GRAHAM BREAD II

¼ cup sugar
¼ cup molasses
1 cup sour milk
1½ cups graham flour

¼ cup white flour
1 teaspoon soda
1 teaspoon baking powder
Salt

1. Sift dry ingredients into bowl.   2. Add liquid, mixing well.   3. Bake about 35 minutes.

Emma D. Hart

GRAPENUT BREAD

½ cup grapenuts
1 cup sour milk
1 scant cup sugar
1 egg

1 teaspoon salt
1 scant teaspoon soda
2 teaspoons baking powder
2 cups flour

1. Let grapenuts stand 10 minutes in sour milk. 2. Sift dry ingredients together. 3. Add beaten egg. 4 Bake in moderate oven 45 minutes.

Mrs. R. H. Watson

NUT BREAD

1 cup sour milk
½ cup maple syrup
1 cup white flour
1 cup graham flour

1½ cup nut meats
1 teaspoon soda
¼ teaspoon salt

1. Sift both kinds of flour, then measure. 2. Add sour milk with soda and maple syrup. 3. Mix well, add nut meats and salt. 4. Bake in moderate oven.

Katherine B. Johnson, Dunkirk

NUT BROWN BREAD

2 cups whole wheat or graham
flour
1 cup white flour
1 cup nuts

1 ½ cups sour milk
½ cup molasses with
1 teaspoon soda
½ teaspoon salt

1. Mix ingredients in order given. 2. Bake 1 hour in slow oven.

Marian Mackie

ORANGE BREAD

Rind of 2 oranges
Water to cover
3 cups flour
4 teaspoons baking powder
1 cup sugar

Salt
1 egg, beaten
1 cup milk
Nuts
1 tablespoon butter, melted

1. Cut the rind of the oranges in small pieces and cover with a little water and boil 5 minutes. 2. Sift the flour, baking powder, salt and sugar into a bowl. 3. Add the milk gradually and the egg. Stir in the nuts and the butter last. 4. Bake in a slow oven.

RAISIN - NUT BREAD

1 egg
1 cup sugar
1 cup milk
3¼ cups flour

1 teaspoon salt
4 teaspoon baking powder
½ cup chopped nuts
1 cup raisins

1. Beat egg, add milk and sugar. 2. Add sifted flour, baking powder and salt. 3. Add nuts and raisins. 4. Pour into greased, paper-lined bread tin. 5. Bake 1½ hours at 300°.

Dorothy T. Clark

STEAMED BROWN BREAD

2 cups sour milk
1 cup brown sugar
Salt
4 tablespoons molasses

4 tablespoons shortening
2 teaspoons soda
1 cup flour
2 cups graham flour

1. Sift dry ingredients in bowl. 2. Add liquid, mixing well. 3. Add melted shortening. 4. Fill coffee cans ¾ full. 5. Steam 2 hours in steamer.

Mary Clothier

COFFEE CAKE
WITH BAKING POWDER . . .

COFFEE CAKE I

1 cup sugar
⅓ cup lard or butter
1 egg
1 cup milk

2 cups flour
2 teaspoons baking powder
Salt
Peanuts

1. Cream the sugar and the shortening and add the egg. Beat well. 2. Sift the flour, baking powder, salt and add alternately with the milk. 3. Sprinkle sugar, cinnamon and chopped peanuts over top before baking. Serve warm.

Clara Wheelock

COFFEE CAKE II

2 eggs well beaten
5 tablespoons sugar
5 tablespoons melted butter

⅔ cup milk
2 cups flour
2 teaspoons baking powder

1. Add the sugar, butter, milk, flour and baking powder to the beaten eggs.
2. Pour into a greased pan. Over the top of the mixture spread melted butter, sugar, and cinnamon. Bake in a moderate oven.

Abbie Walker

KUCHEN

1 cup sugar
1 egg
1 cup sour milk (part sour cream)
2 cups flour
½ teaspoon soda

2 teaspoons baking powder
Salt
1 teaspoon cinnamon
½ teaspoon nutmeg
½ cup raisins

1. Add the egg to the sugar and beat well. 2. Add the soda to the sour milk and add alternately with the sifted flour and baking powder, salt, cinnamon nutmeg and raisins. 3. Pour into a greased and floured baking pan and top with the following before baking:

Kuchen Topping

3 cups brown sugar
1 tablespoon butter

⅓ cup flour
1 cup cocoanut

Mix well and spread over the top of unbaked kuchen and bake until done.

Mary Clothier

HOT BREADS, WAFFLES, GRIDDLE CAKES, ETC. . . .

CORN BREAD

1 cup corn meal (yellow)
1 cup mashed potatoes
3 teaspoons baking powder
2 tablespoons sugar

⅓ teaspoon salt
¾ cup milk
2 tablespoons bacon fat
1 egg

1. Mix in order given.   2. Melt bacon fat in pan in which bread is to be baked but pour melted fat into batter.   3. Bake about ½ hour in 375° oven.

Mrs. B. H. Ritenburg

DIXIE SPOON BREAD

2 cups milk
1 cup southern corn meal (white)

½ teaspoon salt
4 eggs

1. Scald milk.   2. Slowly stir in sifted corn meal.   3. Add salt and let boil 2 or 3 minutes.   4. Remove from fire and add beaten egg yolks.   5. Beat well, then add the stiffly beaten egg whites.   6. Pour into hot buttered baking dish or pan and bake in moderate oven ½ hour.   7. Serve immediately from pan or dish in which it is cooked.

Cora Sawyer Scott

BLUEBERRY MUFFINS

½ cup sugar
2 tablespoons soft shortening
1 egg
1 cup milk

2 cups flour
3 teaspoons baking powder
1 full cup blueberries
½ teaspoon salt

1. Sift a little flour on blueberries. 2. Mix ingredients adding blueberries last. 3. Fill tins half full.   4. Oven at 400°, then turn to 375°.   5. Bake 30 minutes.

Ida Weaver

CORN MUFFINS

1 cup yellow corn meal
1 cup white flour
1 cup sweet or sour milk
½ cup sugar

1 egg
2 large tablespoons melted Butter
Salt

If sweet milk is used — 2 teaspoons baking powder;   If sour milk is used — ½ teaspoon soda and 1 teaspoon baking pwoder.
1. Sift dry ingredients.   2. Add milk, then shortening. Bake in moderate oven.

Mary Heffernan

GRAHAM MUFFINS

1 beaten egg
½ cup sugar
1 cup sour milk
1 ½ cups graham flour

1 teaspoon soda
2 tablespoons melted butter
¼ teaspoon salt

1. Add soda to sour milk. 2. Sift dry ingredients. 3. Add liquid, beaten egg. 4. Add melted butter. 5. Bake in moderate oven 425º—20 minutes.

Mrs. Robert K. Pierce

MUFFINS

¼ cup shortening
¼ cup sugar
1 beaten egg
1 cup milk

1¾ cups flour
½ teaspoon salt
4 teaspoons baking powder

1. Sift dry ingredients. 2. Add liquid. 3. Add beaten egg 4. Add melted shortening. 5 Bake in quick oven.

Clara Wheelock

RICE MUFFINS

2 ¼ cups flour
¾ cup cooked rice
4 teaspoons baking powder
2 tablespoons melted butter

1 cup milk
1 egg
Salt

1. Sift dry ingredients. 2. Mix in milk, rice. 3. Add beaten egg, then shortening. 4. Bake in muffin tins in moderate oven.

Mary S. Strunk

HIGHLAND SCONES

Blend
5 tablespoons melted shortening with
2 cups bread flour
2 tablespoons sugar

4 teaspoons baking powder
½ teaspoon salt
½ cup milk
2 eggs

1. Sift the flour, sugar, baking powder and salt. 2. Stir in milk and eggs. 3. Spoon onto oiled paper dusted with flour. Pat into 1-4 inch thickness. 4. Spread half the dough with raspberry jam. Cover with other half. 5. Brush with milk. 6. Cut into squares, then triangles. 7. Bake 15 minutes in hot oven. To serve with salad, omit sugar and spread with ¾ cup grated cheese in place of jam.

Thera D. Wood

SCONES

2 cups flour
2 teaspoons baking powder
½ cup sugar
½ cup butter

Pinch salt
1 egg in cup and fill with milk
½ cup raisins in the flour

1. Mix dry ingredients. 2. Add liquid, then melted shortening. 3. Roll like biscuit, cut in squares about 3 inches thick. Fold cornerwise and bake in quick oven.

Mrs. B. H. Ritenburg

BAKING POWDER BISCUITS I

2 cups flour
3 teaspoons baking powder
½ teaspoon salt

4 tablespoons shortening
½ cup water
1 egg

1. Cream shortening.   2. Add dry ingredients sifted.   3. Add liquid.   4. Add beaten egg.   5. Bake at 450o for 12 minutes.

Laura McKale

BAKING POWDER BISCUITS II

2 cups flour
4 level teaspoons baking pow-
    der
½ cup shortening
½ cup sweet milk

½ cup buttermilk
Salt
Scant ½ teaspoon soda in
buttermilk

1. Cream shortening.   2. Add dry ingredients sifted.   3. Add buttermilk with soda, sweet milk.   4. Bake at 450o for 12 minutes.

Mrs. James Rowan

APPLE FRITTERS

2 cups pastry flour
1 teaspoon baking powder
1 teaspoon sugar
1 teaspoon salt

3 eggs
6 ripe apples
½ cup milk
1 tablespoon fat

1. Peel and core apples. Cut in quarters.   2. Beat eggs, add fat, then milk, then all dry ingredients sifted together. 3. Dip each piece of apple in batter and fry until soft in deep fat (375o - 385o).

Mrs. Fred Bullock

CORN FRITTERS

1 cup flour
2 eggs
¾ teaspoon salt
1 teaspoon baking powder

2 teaspoons melted butter
1½ cups drained, canned corn
    or fresh corn cut from cob

1. Sift dry ingredients.   2. Beat eggs, add milk and combine with first mixture. Beat thoroughly.   3. Add corn and melted butter.   4. Drop by tablespoon into deep hot fat (360o - 370o F.).

Mrs. Fred Bullock

CHEESE STRAWS

1½ cups grated American cheese
½ cup butter
2½ cups flour

1 teaspoon salt
Pinch of cayenne pepper

1. Work flour and butter with tips of fingers.   2. Add cheese moistened with water. 3. Toss on slightly floured board and knead. 4. Roll into ⅛ inch thickness. 5. Cut in strips four to five inches long. 6. Bake about 20 minutes.

Cora Sawyer Scott

SNITZ and KNEP

1 pound dried apple snits
1 pound bacon
3 cups flour
3 teaspoons baking powder

Salt
2 eggs
Milk

1. Soak apple snits 2 hours. 2. Place in kettle of water with bacon and boil 1½ hours (covered). 3. Make stiff batter of flour, baking powder, salt, eggs, milk. 4. Drop by spoonfuls into kettle and cover. 5. Boil 20 minutes and be sure there is enough water in kettle so knep will not burn.

Edna Foss.

WHIPPED CREAM WAFFLES

1 cup heavy cream
2 teaspoons sugar
2 cups flour
½ cup heavy cream (use as much as needed to thin batter)
2 eggs, separated
2 tablespoons melted butter
½ teaspoon salt

1. Whip cream. 2. Beat egg yolks and add. 3. Add dry ingredients. 4. Add enough heavy cream to make batter thin to spread on iron. 5. Fold in beaten egg whites.

Norrine Walker

WAFFLES I

2 eggs
1¼ cups milk
2 cups flour
4 teaspoons baking powder
¼ teaspoon salt
8 tablespoons melted butter

1. Add milk to slightly beaten egg yolks. 2. Add flour sifted with baking powder and salt. 3. Mix well and add melted butter. 4. Fold in stiffly beaten egg whites.

Margaret Gregory

WAFFLES II

1 cup cream, whipped
(sweet or sour)
1 egg
1 teaspoon baking powder
1 cup sifted Swans Down flour
4 teaspoons melted butter

1. If sour cream is used add pinch of soda. 2. Add beaten yolk of egg, flour and baking powder. 3. Add melted butter. 4. Add beaten egg white.

Mrs. Fred Aten, Goodland, Kansas

BUCKWHEAT GRIDDLE CAKES

⅓ yeast cake dissolved in
⅓ cup lukewarm water
⅓ cup corn meal
1 tablespoon molasses
Salt
Pinch mustard
1 cup wheat flour
2 cups buckwheat flour
Warm water or sour milk

1. Mix well with water or sour milk to make thick batter. 2. Set in warm place over night. 3. In the morning, add salt and soda in water. 4. Add more warm water to make batter thin enough to pour. 5. Cook as regular griddle cakes. One cup of batter may be used for a second mixing to substitute for yeast.

Mrs. E. W. Schneider

BUCKWHEAT CAKES

⅓ cup dried bread crumbs
2 cups scalded milk
¼ cake yeast dissolved in
¼ cup lukewarm water

1¾ cups buckwheat flour
1 tablespoon molasses
¼ teaspoon soda

1. Pour milk over crumbs and let stand 30 minutes. 2. Add salt, dissolved yeast, buckwheat flour to make thin enough batter to pour. 3. Let rise over night. Stir well, add molasses and soda in ¼ cup lukewarm water. 5. Cook as regular griddle cakes.

Mrs. E. W. Schneider

RHODE ISLAND JOHNNY CAKES

1 cup corn meal
1 tablespoon flour (heaping)

1 ½ cups sweet milk

1. Scald ½ cup meal with a little boiling water. 2. Add a little of milk to cool 3. Add flour and other ½ cup meal. Mix well. 4. Bake on well-greased griddle. Do not try to turn until browned. These will be very thin.

Abbie Walker

SOUTHERN GRIDDLE CAKES

4 cups flour
4 teaspoon baking powder
1 teaspoon salt
3 tablespoons sugar

3 cups milk
4 eggs
4 tablespoons melted butter

1. Sift flour, salt, sugar, baking powder. 2. Add milk and egg yolks, melted butter. 3. Beat well, then add the stiffly beaten egg whites. 4. Bake on hot greased griddle.

Helen Cowden

CAKES . . .

ANGEL FOOD CAKE

1 cup sifted cake flour	1 teaspoon cream tartar
1¼ cups egg white	¾ teaspoon vanilla
¼ teaspoon salt	¼ teaspoon almond extract
1¼ cups sifted sugar	3 tablespoons cold water

1. Sift flour once; measure; sift flour four more times. 2. Beat egg whites, water and salt with flat wire whisk. 3. When foamy, add cream of tartar and continue beating until eggs are stiff enough to hold up in peaks, but not dry. 4. Fold in sugar, 2 tablespoons at a time. 5. Add flavoring. 6. Then add flour in small amounts and fold in until all is used. 7. Turn into ungreased angel food pan and put in cold oven 8. Increase heat gradually until oven temperature reaches 275º for about 30 minutes. 9. Then increase heat to 325º for last 30 minutes. 10. Remove from oven and invert pan 1 hour, or until cake is cold.

Rhea Stevens

APRICOT SUSHINE CAKE

1 cup cake flour	½ cup apricot juice (canned or freshly stewed)
¾ teaspoon cream of tartar	
¼ teaspoon salt	6 egg whites beaten stiffly
1 ½ cups sugar	6 egg yolks beaten until thick and lemon colored

1. Sift flour once; measure; add cream of tartar and salt. 2. Sift three or four times. 3. Boil sugar and apricot juice until it spins a thread. 4. Pour hot syrup in a fine stream on beaten egg whites, beating constantly until mixture cools. 5. Fold in beaten egg yolks. 6. Fold in flour a small quantity at a time. 7. Pour into an ungreased angel cake pan. 8. Bake in a moderate oven 1 hour (350º). 9. Remove from oven and invert pan to cool.

Katherine Regan Kane, Dunkirk

BANANA CAKE

4 tablespoons shortening	1 cup mashed bananas (4 small bananas)
1 ½ cups sugar	
2 eggs	¼ cup sour milk
¾ teaspoon soda	1 teaspoon vanilla
½ teaspoon baking powder	1 ½ cups flour

1. Cream shortening and add sugar and cream. 2. Mash bananas with a fork and add gradually to the above mixture. 3. Add eggs and then sour milk in which the soda has been dissolved. 4. Sift the flour and baking powder and add. 5. Stir in vanilla. 6. Bake in three layers in a moderate oven (350º to 375º) for 30 minutes. 7. Put together with Seven Minute Icing and put sliced bananas between layers, and a few on top.

Mabel Hanson

BLACK CHOCOLATE CAKE

1½ cups granulated sugar	½ cup sweet milk
½ cup butter	1 teaspoon soda
3 eggs	2 cups flour
½ cup grated chocolate	Vanilla

1. Cream butter and sugar. .2 Add beaten eggs. 3. Sift soda and flour and add. 4. Add vanilla. 5. Cook grated chocolate in milk and when thoroughly cold, add to cake mixture. 6. Bake at 350°.

May Hayward

CHOCOLATE CAKE I

1 cup light brown sugar	1 teaspoon soda
¼ cup butter	1 large cup flour
1 egg	4 teaspoons cocoa
½ cup buttermilk	½ cup boiling water

1. Cream butter and sugar. 2. Add beaten egg. 3. Dissolve soda in buttermilk and add. 4. Dissolve cocoa in boiling water and add alternately with sifted flour. 5. Bake at 350° for loaf cake and 375° for layer cake.

Elizabeth Stevens

CHOCOLATE CAKE II

1 cup sugar	1 teaspoon vanilla
1 tablespoon butter	1 teaspoon soda
½ cup milk	(little more than level)
1 ½ cups flour	½ cup milk boiled with
1 egg	2 squares chocolate

1. Mix sugar and butter. 2. Add beaten egg. 3. Sift flour and soda and add alternately with milk. 4. Add vanilla and then the ½ cup milk in which chocolate has been boiled. 5. Bake at 350°.

Leora Weiss

CHOCOLATE ROLL

6 eggs, beaten separately	6 tablespoons powdered sugar
3 tablespoons grated bitter chocolate, melted	Pinch of salt

1. Add sugar to the egg yolks and beat until creamy. 2. Add the chocolate, and salt and fold in stiffly beaten whites. 3. Bake in a square flat pan, which has been buttered and floured, for 5 minutes in a hot oven (400°). 4. Turn out on brown paper sprinkled with sugar. 5. Roll while hot and cover with damp cloth. Cool. 6. When ready to serve, unroll and spread with chocolate frosting, then whipped cream on top of the frosting. 7. Reroll and serve with more whipped cream.

Dora Cease

CHOCOLATE NUT CAKE

1 cup sugar	1 teaspoon soda
½ cup shortening	2 cups flour
3 tablespoons cocoa	½ teaspoon salt
½ cup boiling water	1 cup walnut meats
½ cup sour milk	1 teaspoon vanilla

1. Cream sugar and shortening. 2. Dissolve cocoa in boiling water, and add. 3. Combine soda and sour milk and add. 4. Sift salt and flour into mixture and stir in the nuts and vanilla. 5. Bake 1 hour at 325°.

Mrs. Louise L. Phillips

Get a "million-dollar" cake — every time!

YOU CAN.. but not with ordinary flour!

How are you at cake-baking? . . . Do you always feel as proud as you'd like to feel? . . . Or do you sometimes shake your head sadly?

This page is here to show you how to make *far better* cake than you ever have before. How to get *smoother, lighter texture —a tenderer delicacy—a "million-dollar"* cake every time!

Here is how!—instead of ordinary flour, use Swans Down Cake Flour!

You may wonder how flour, *and just flour,* can matter so much. But make the test to-day. Try the delicious, brand-new Devil's Food on the back of this page. Or use any cake-recipe in this book. Just be sure to use Swans Down—

and see if you don't say, "*I never made such perfect cake with ordinary flour.*"

Swans Down's secret is simple enough. Ordinary flour, you see, contains a tenacious, elastic gluten. It takes this kind of gluten to withstand the mixing and kneading of bread dough.

But Swans Down is made from the choicest wheat grown. The Swans Down gluten is unusually tender—so delicate that it responds perfectly to "quick" cake leavens, and gives extra lightness to any cake.

And Swans Down Cake Flour is 27 times finer than ordinary flour!

Get Swans Down at your grocer's today. It is a product of General Foods.

PRIZE DEVIL'S FOOD CAKE

2 cups sifted Swans Down Cake Flour	3 eggs, well beaten
2¾ teaspoons baking powder	3 squares Baker's Unsweetened Chocolate, melted
¼ teaspoon salt	
⅔ cup butter or other shortening	¾ cup milk
1½ cups sugar	1 teaspoon vanilla

Sift flour once, measure, add baking powder and salt, and sift together three times. Cream butter thoroughly, add sugar gradually, and cream together until light and fluffy. Add eggs and beat well; then chocolate and blend. Add flour, alternately with milk, a small amount at a time, beating after each addition until smooth. Add vanilla. Bake in two greased 9-inch layer pans in moderate oven (350° F.) 30 minutes, or until done. Spread Fruit Nut Filling between layers and Ivory Frosting on top and sides of cake. Double recipe to make three 10-inch layers.

FRUIT NUT FILLING

⅓ cup chopped dates
⅓ cup chopped raisins
¾ cup sugar
1 cup water
⅓ cup broken walnut meats
1 tablespoon lemon juice
1 teaspoon grated lemon rind

Combine dates, raisins, sugar, and water in saucepan. Cook over low flame 15 minutes, or until thick enough to spread, stirring constantly. Cool; add nuts, lemon juice and rind. Chill before spreading. Makes enough filling to spread between two 9-inch layers.

All measurements are level.

IVORY FROSTING

2 egg whites, unbeaten
¼ cup brown sugar, firmly packed
1¼ cups granulated sugar
5 tablespoons water
1 teaspoon vanilla

Combine egg whites, sugars, and water in top of double boiler, beating with rotary egg beater until thoroughly mixed. Place over rapidly boiling water, beat constantly with rotary egg beater, and cook 7 minutes, or until frosting will stand in peaks. Remove from boiling water; add vanilla and beat until thick enough to spread. Makes enough frosting to cover top and sides of two 9-inch layers generously.

Send for this
SWANS DOWN CAKE SET . . . it's a bargain!

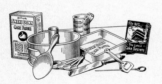

CRUMB CAKE I

2 eggs
2 cups flour
1 ½ cups brown sugar
½ cup butter

1 cup sour milk
1 teaspoon soda
½ teaspoon spices (cinnamon, cloves and nutmeg mixed)

1. Mix sugar, butter and flour. 2. Take out ½ cup of this mixture for top. 3. To the remainder add milk, soda, eggs and spices. 4. Put this mixture in well-greased pan about 7x11. 5. Sprinkle the ½ cup of first mixture evenly over the top. 6. Bake in a moderate oven — 350°.

Mrs. Bruce Ritenburg

CRUMB CAKE II

1 cup sugar
½ cup butter
2 cups flour
½ cup milk

3 teaspoons baking powder
2 eggs
1 teaspoon vanilla

1 Sift all the dry ingredients together. 2. Add butter and mix thoroughly with the hands. 3. Put aside one-half cup of crumbs. 4. Beat eggs very light, add to the milk and beat into the dry mixture gradually. 5. Bake in a shallow pan and cover the top with the half cup of crumbs. (350°).

Emily G. Hayward

CUP CAKES

1 cup sugar
3 level tablespoons butter
2 egg yolks
1 teaspoon soda

1 cup sour milk or buttermilk
1 ½ cups cake flour
2 teaspoon baking powder
1 teaspoon vanilla

1. Cream butter and sugar. 2. Add beaten egg yolks. 3. Dissolve soda in milk and add. 4. Sift baking powder with flour and add to above mixture. 5. Add vanilla. 6. Bake 375° to 400°.

Rhea Stevens

DATE CAKE

1 package dates, cut up
1 teaspoon soda
½ cup nut meats
1 cup boiling water
1 cup sugar
¾ cup shortening

1 egg
1½ cups flour
1 teaspoon baking powder
Salt
Vanilla

1. Add the soda to the boiling water and pour over the dates. Cool. 2. Cream the sugar and shortening and add the beaten egg. 3. Combine the two mixtures and stir in the sifted four, baking powder and salt. 4. Add the vanilla and the nuts. 5. Bake in a moderate oven (350°) 45 to 50 minutes.

Leah Phillips

DEVIL'S FOOD CAKE I

Part 1
1 cup brown sugar
3 tablespoons cocoa
½ cup water
Part 2
1 cup brown sugar

½ cup shortening
2 eggs
½ cup water
2 cups flour
1 teaspoon soda
1 teaspoon baking powder

1. Boil ingredients in Part 1 and set aside to cool. 2. Cream sugar and shortening.   3. Add beaten eggs.   4. Sift flour, soda and baking powder and add alternately with water.   5. Add Part 2 to Part 1 and bake at 350°.

Mrs. Cleveland Dietzen, Dunkirk

DEVIL'S FOOD CAKE II

1 cup sugar
¼ cup melted shortening
¼ cup sour milk
1 teaspoon baking powder
1 teaspoon soda
1 egg

½ boiling water
¼ cup cocoa
1 large cup flour
¼ teaspoon salt
1 teaspoon vanilla

1. Cream sugar and shortening together.   2. Add beaten egg.   3. Dissolve soda in sour milk and add.   4. Sift baking powder, flour and salt together and add alternately with the cocoa dissolved in water.   5. Pour in 8-inch tin and bake at 350° to 375°.

Mrs. Charles Grover

DEVIL'S FOOD CAKE III

½ cup butter
1 cup sugar
1 egg
1½ squares chocolate
¼ cup boiling water

1½ cups cake flour
1 teaspoon vinegar
Milk
Vanilla
1 teaspoon soda

1. Cream butter and sugar, and add beaten egg.   2. Make paste of chocolate and water, and when cool, add vinegar, soda and enough milk to make a full cup, and stir into butter and sugar mixture.   3. Add sifted cake flour, mixing well.   4. Bake at 375° for 25 minutes. This makes a very moist, delicious cake and is handy, if one fails to have sour milk on hand.

Mildred Rogger

DEVIL'S FOOD WITH MOLASSES

1 cup sugar
½ cup butter
2 eggs
1 teaspoon soda
2 squares chocolate

1 cup sour milk
½ cup molasses
1¾ cups flour
1 teaspoon cinnamon
¾ teaspoon nutmeg

1. Cream butter and sugar. 2. Add well beaten eggs. 3. Melt chocolate over warm water, and add. 4. Dissolve soda in sour milk and add. 5. Add molasses, mixing thoroughly. 6. Then add flour and spices sifted together. 7. Bake in a moderate oven (375°).

Mrs. Willard G. Conaway

FEATHER SPICE CAKE

2½ cups flour
2½ teaspoons baking powder
¼ teaspoon salt
1 teaspoon cinnamon
½ teaspoon mace
¼ teaspoon cloves

½ cup butter
1 cup sugar
2 eggs, unbeaten
⅓ cup molasses
¾ cup milk

1. Sift flour once, measure, add baking powder, salt and spices, and sift three times. 2. Cream butter, add sugar and cream together until light and fluffy. 3. Add eggs, unbeaten. 4 Add molasses, and blend. 5. Add flour mixture alternately with milk. 6. Bake at 375° for 30 minutes.

Mrs. Harry Schwartz

FOUR EGG SPONGE CAKE

4 eggs
1½ cups sugar
½ cup boiling water
1¾ cups flour

½ teaspoon cream of tartar
½ teaspoon baking powder
1 teaspoon vanilla
Salt

1. Beat egg whites until they begin to froth, add cream of tartar and continue beating until stiff, but not dry. 2. Beat egg yolks until thick and lemon colored. 3. Add sugar gradually to egg yolks. Add hot water and vanilla. 5. Sift baking powder, salt and flour five times and add. 6. Fold in egg whites. 7. Bake in tube pan, ungreased, at 300° for ½ hour and at 325° for ½ hour.

Virginia Morrison

FRUIT CAKE (STEAMED)

1 cup butter
2 cups sugar
3½ cups flour
1 cup sour cream
1 cup molasses
4 eggs

2 pounds raisins
¼ pound citron
1 pound currants
2 teaspoons soda
Spices to taste
Nuts, if desired

1.Cream butter and sugar. 2. Add beaten eggs. 3. Add molasses, and the soda dissolved in sour cream. 4. Add flour, fruit, and spices and nuts. 5. Mix and steam three hours. 6. Then bake in slow oven 45 minutes.

Helen Price Cowden

FRUIT CAKE

1 pound (1⅔ cups) mince-
    meat
1 cup nuts
1 cup raisins
½ cup melted butter
1 cup sugar

2 cups flour
2 egg yolks
1 teaspoon soda
1 teaspoon boiling water
Vanilla
2 egg whites

1. Mix butter and sugar. 2. Add beaten egg yolks. 3. Dissolve soda in water and add alternately with flour. 4. Add mince-meat, chopped nuts, raisins and vanilla. 5. Add beaten egg whites. 6. Bake 1 hour in moderate oven (350°).

Margaret Gailewicz

FRUIT CUP CAKES

½ cup butter
1 cup sugar
1 cup sour cream
2 cups cake flour
2 eggs
2 teaspoons cinnamon
2 teaspoons nutmeg

½ teaspoon cloves
1 teaspoon soda
½ cup chopped nuts
½ cup chopped dates
½ cup candied cherries
½ cup candied pineapple

1. Cream butter and sugar.   2. Add soda dissolved in sour cream, and beaten eggs.   3. Sift flour and spices; add fruit and nuts; and add to cake mixture. 4. Bake in cup cake tins at 375°.

Mary Howells

GINGER CAKE

2 eggs	½ teaspoon cloves
½ cup sugar	½ teaspoon cinnamon
1 cup shortening	1 teaspoon soda
1 cup molasses	2 teaspoons baking powder
1 cup boiling water	1 teaspoon ginger
2½ cups flour	

1. Beat eggs, add sugar and shortening and cream thoroughly.   2. Add water and soda to molasses and add to above alternately with flour, baking powder and spices sifted together.   3. Bake slowly — about 300°.

Mrs. Leslie Wolford, Dunkirk

GINGER BREAD

⅔ cup butter	1 teaspoon ginger
1 cup molasses	2½ cups flour
2 eggs	2 level teaspoons soda
1 cup brown sugar	1 cup boiling water
2 teaspoons cinnamon	

1. Cream butter and brown sugar. 2. Add well beaten eggs.   3. Dissolve soda in water and add along with molasses.   4. Sift flour and spices and add, mixing well. 5. Bake slowly, 350° then turn down to 300°. 6. This will make one very large cake or two medium size.   It may seem thin when stirred together, but needs no more flour.

May Hayward

JAPANESE CAKE

½ cup butter	1 teaspoon cinnamon
1 cup sugar	½ teaspoon cloves
Yolks 2 eggs	1 cup boiling water
3 tablespoons molasses	1 level teaspoon soda
2 cups flour	

1. Mix butter and sugar.   2. Add egg yolks and molasses.   3. Sift flour and spices and dissolve soda in water. adding alternately to above.   4. Bake in moderate oven, 350° to 375°. 5. Frost with Seven Minute Icing, to which add chopped dates.

JELLY ROLL

4 eggs	1 cup cake flour
1 cup sugar	1½ teaspoons baking powder
1½ tablespoons cornstarch	Salt
3 tablespoons cold water	Vanilla

1. Beat egg yolk. 2. Add sugar and remaining ingredients. 3. Add beaten egg whites last. 4. Bake quickly in well greased, shallow tin. 5. When slightly warm, turn from tin onto board covered with confectioners sugar. 6. Spread

with jelly or jam and roll.   If edges are too crisp, they must be removed with sharp knife before rolling.

Clara Wheelock

LEMON SPONGE CAKE

1½ cups milk	5 tablespoons lemon juice
1 cup sugar	Grated rind of 1 lemon
3 eggs	4 tablespoons flour
2 tablespoons butter	Salt

1. Cream butter, add sugar, flour, salt and lemon juice and rind.   2. Stir in beaten egg yolks mixed with milk.   3. Fold in egg whites.   4. Pour into custard cups or pudding pan, set in a pan of water, and bake about 45 minutes in a moderate oven.   When done, each cup will contain custard at the bottom and sponge cake on top.

MAPLE NUT CAKE

⅓ cup shortening	2 teaspoons baking powder
1 cup light brown sugar	1 teaspoon vanilla
2 egg yolks	½ teaspoon salt
¾ cup milk	1 cup chopped nuts
1½ cups flour	

1. Cream shortening and sugar.   2. Add well beaten egg yolks.   3. Sift flour, baking powder and salt and add to the above with milk and nuts.   4 Add vanilla and mix thoroughly.   5. Bake in a moderate oven.

Mary Howells

MATRIMONIAL CAKE

Part 1	Part 2
1 pound dates	1½ cups flour
½ cup sugar	1¼ cups oatmeal
1½ cups water	¾ cup butter
	1 cup brown sugar
	½ teaspoon soda
	½ teaspoon salt

1. Blend butter and sugar.   2. Add salt, soda, flour and oatmeal.   3. Pat one-half of Part 2 mixture into tin.   4. Put Part 1 mixture in smooth layer over it.   5. Then add the other half of Part 2 mixture.   6. Bake 20 minutes in moderate oven, 350°. 7. Cut in squares before cold.   A package of mince-meat makes an excellent filling.

Mrs. Forrest Cummings, Dunkirk

MOCK ANGEL FOOD CAKE (Outdoor Recipe)

1 loaf unsliced white bread	½ pound fresh cocoanut
1 can sweetened condensed milk	

1. Cut crusts from bread and cut in 3-inch cubes.   2. Spread thickly with milk and roll in cocoanut.   3. Toast lightly on end of stick.   These can be toasted in oven.

Esther Oaks

MOROCCO CHOCOLATE CAKE

2½ cups sifted cake flour
1 teaspoon baking powder
½ teaspoon soda
½ teaspoon salt
½ cup butter

2 cups sugar
3 eggs, well beaten
4 square chocolate, melted
1 cup water
1 teaspoon vanilla

1. Sift flour once, measure, add baking powder, soda and salt and sift 3 times. 2. Cream the butter, add sugar gradually creaming well. 3. Add eggs and beat well. 4. Add chocolate and blend. 5. Add flour alternately with the water in small amounts, beating after each addition. Add vanilla. 6. Bake in 2 9-inch pans at 350° for 30 minutes.

Raisin, Nut Morocco Frosting:

1. Mix well in top of double boiler—2 unbeaten egg whites, 1 1-4 cups granulated sugar, 1-4 cup firmly packed brown sugar. 2. Add 5 tablespoons water, beat 7 minutes or until it stands in peaks. 3. Remove from water, add 1 cup cut raisins, 1 cup broken walnut meats, 1-2 teaspoon grated lemon rind. 4. Fold in carefully 1-2 or 1 square chocolate melted.

Mrs. J. B. Schoeffel

NUT CAKE

½ cup butter (scant)
1½ cups sugar
2 cups cake flour
2 teaspoons baking powder

¾ cup milk
1 cup chopped nutmeats
Whites of 4 eggs

1. Cream butter and sugar. 2. Sift flour before measuring, sift with baking powder, and add to above alternately with milk. 3. Add chopped nuts and the egg whites beaten stiff. 4. Bake at 350° in 9-inch square pan for 45 minutes.

Louise Klopfer.

OLD FASHIONED ENGLISH CARRAWAY SEED CAKE

6 ounces flour
4 ounces sugar
¼ teaspoon baking powder
A little milk

4 ounces butter
2 eggs
1 teaspoon carraway seeds
Pinch of salt

1. Sieve the flour, baking powder and pinch of salt together, and add the carraway seeds. 2. Put the butter and sugar in a basin and cream until pale in color, then beat in each egg separately. 3. Stir in the sieved flour, adding a little milk to make the mixture the correct consistency. 4. Put into a prepared cake tin and bake at a temperature of 360° for approximately 1 hour.

Jane Potter.

ORANGE CAKE

1½ cups sugar
1 cup shortening
2 eggs
1½ cups sour milk
1 teaspoon soda
3 cups flour

Salt
1 teaspoon baking powder
1 cup chopped nuts
1 cup raisins and 1 whole
orange, ground together

1. Cream shortening and sugar. 2. Add well beaten eggs. 3. Dissolve soda in sour milk and add alternately with sifted dry ingredients. 4. Add chopped nuts, and the raisins and orange ground together. 5. Bake in a slow oven, 325º to 350º. 6. Ice with a plain icing or serve with whipped cream.

Esther Rabin.

ORANGE FILLED CAKE

½ cup shortening
1 cup sugar
2 whole eggs
1¾ cups cake flour

½ teaspoon salt
2 teaspoons baking powder
½ cup cold water
Orange flavoring

1. Cream shortening and sugar. 2. Add beaten eggs. 3. Sift flour, salt and baking powder, and add alternately with cold water and orange extract. 4. Bake in layer pans about 375º.

Filling

2 egg yolks
3 tablespoons sugar
2 tablespoons flour

Orange flavoring
1 cup milk

1. Mix above ingredients and cook until thick. 2. Cool and put between cake layers. 3. Use any white icing receipe and flavor with orange.

Mrs. Robert Gardner.

ORANGE ROLL

4 eggs
1 cup sugar
1 teaspoon baking powder
1 cup sifted flour

¼ teaspoon salt
5 tablespoons hot water
2 teaspoons lemon juice

1. Beat eggs and sugar together until mixture is very stiff and light. 2. Add lemon juice and sifted dry ingredients alternately with hot water. 3. Pour into well-buttered jelly cake pan and bake in 400º oven for 12 minutes. 4. Turn onto waxed paper. 5. Spread with prepared mixture and roll immediately. 6. Cool and slice and serve with whipped cream.

Orange Filling

⅔ cup apricot pulp
⅔ cup sugar

2 tablespoons grated orange rind
2 tablespoons orange juice

1. Add sugar to thick apricot puree. 2. Cook until mixture is thick and clear. 3. Remove from fire and add orange juice and rind. 4. Cool and spread on hot cake.

Mary Heffernan.

ORANGE SPONGE CAKE

1¼ cups sugar
5 tablespoon boiling water
6 egg whites
½ teaspoon cream tartar

6 egg yolks
1 cup flour
½ teaspoon vanilla

1. Boil sugar and water until it threads. 2. Beat egg whites partly and add

cream of tartar and beat stiff.   3. Add syrup gradually and beat until cool.
4. Beat egg yolks, add vanilla, and fold into first mixure.   5. Fold in flour.
6. Bake 50 minutes in the tube pan in slow oven.

Icing

2 cups sugar
1 cup water
2 tablespoons white corn syrup

Grated rind 1 orange
1 tablespoon lemon juice

1. Cook sugar, water and corn syrup together until 252o or a hard ball.   2. Pour
hot syrup over fruit mixture.   3. Cool and beat.

Norinne Walker.

PINEAPPLE CAKE

½ cup butter
1 cup sugar
2 eggs
1 small can crushed pineapple
2 cups flour

2 teaspoons baking powder
1 teaspoon soda
1 teaspoon cinnamon
1 cup chopped dates and nuts

1. Cream butter and sugar.   2. Beat eggs and add   3. Add crushed pineapple
and mix well.   4. Sift flour, baking powder, soda and cinnamon and add.
5. Last add chopped dates and nuts and mix thoroughly. 6. Bake about 40
minutes at 350o.   7. Serve with whipped cream.

Esther Rabin.

RED CHOCOLATE CAKE

2 cups brown sugar
½ cup butter
2 eggs
½ cup sour milk
1 teaspoon vanilla

1 teaspoon soda
2 cups cake flour
½ cup cocoa
½ cup hot water

1. Cream butter and sugar.   2. Add beaten eggs.   3. Dissolve soda in sour milk
and add alternately with sifted flour.   4. Dissolve cocoa in hot water and add.
5. Add vanilla.   6. Bake at 350o. — This makes a large cake.

Marguerite Taft.

SANATORIAN CAKE

4 egg yolks
1½ cups sugar
½ cup butter
1 cup sour milk
4 tablespoons molasses
2½ cups cake flour

1 teaspoon soda
1 teaspoon cinnamon
¼ teaspoon nutmeg
¼ teaspoon cloves
¼ teaspoon salt

1. Beat egg yolks until thick and lemon colored. 2. Gradually add sugar and
beat until smooth. 3. Add butter, sour milk and molasses. 4. Add flour sifted
with soda, spices and salt, and mix until smooth. 5. Place in greased and floured
cake pans and bake at 350o to 375o for 30 minutes. Cool and put together with
the following icing:

Icing

4 egg whites	1 cup chopped raisins
Confectioners' sugar	

1. Beat egg whites stiffly.   2. Add confectioners' sugar until the mixture is the desired consistency for spreading.   3. Add chopped raisins.

Inez M. Ransom.

SOUR CREAM CAKE

2 eggs	1 teaspoon baking powder
1 cup sour cream	(rounding)
1 cup white sugar	Salt
1½ cup flour	Vanilla
½ teaspoon soda	

1. Beat eggs; add sugar and beat well.   2. Mix soda and sour cream and add to sugar and eggs. 3. Add flour, baking powder and salt sifted together. 4. Add vanilla and mix well.   5. Bake in layers in a moderate oven.

Mary Dunbar.

SPANISH SPONGE CAKE

2 cups cake flour	1 cup sugar
1 teaspoon soda	2 eggs
1 teaspoon baking powder	1 cup sour milk
2 teaspoons cinnamon	1 cup brown sugar
½ cup shortening	1 cup walnuts

1. Measure flour, add soda, baking powder and cinnamon and sift three times. 2. Cream shortening, add sugar gradually, creaming well.   3. Add beaten egg yolks and mix thoroughly.   4. Add flour mixture alternately with sour milk. 5. Beat the egg whites stiff. Add brown sugar and broken nutmeats and spread on top of cake.   6. Bake in moderate oven (350°) for one hour.

Ruth Bremer.

SPICE CAKE

1 cup brown sugar	1½ cups flour
½ cup butter	1 cup sour milk
1 teaspoon cinnamon	2 small teaspoons soda
1 teaspoon cloves	1 cup raisins and nuts

1. Cream butter and add sugar.   2. Add egg well beaten.   3. Dissolve soda in sour milk and add alternately with the flour and spices sifted together.   4. Add raisins and nuts and mix well.   5. Bake at 350° for about 45 minutes.

Mrs. F. E. Brockett.

SPICED FRUIT CUP CAKES

½ cup butter	1 cup sour milk
1 cup brown sugar	1 teaspoon soda
2 eggs	2¼ cups flour
1 cup raisins or dates	2 teaspoon baking powder
1 orange, ground	½ teaspoon cinnamon
½ cup nuts	¼ teaspoon cloves

1. Cream butter and sugar together. 2. Add beaten eggs and beat mixture well. 3. Add raisins, orange and chopped nuts. 4. Add alternately the soda dissolved in sour milk and the dry ingredients sifted together. 5. Bake about 20 minutes in 370° oven.

Eva Clark.

SPICED CUP CAKES

1 cup sugar
½ cup bacon drippings
(use some butter)
2 eggs
⅔ cup milk
1 tablespoon molasses
3 teaspoons baking powder
1 teaspoon cinnamon

½ teaspoon cloves
½ teaspoon allspice
¼ teaspoon ginger
½ teaspoon salt
2 cups flour
1 cup cut raisins
1 teaspoon vanilla

1. Cream sugar and shortening. 2. Stir in the eggs and beat well. 3. Add the molasses. 4. Sift dry ingredients together and add alternately with the milk. 5. Fold in raisins and add the vanilla. 6. Bake in muffin tins at 350° for 25 minutes.

Cecile Szpaks

SPONGE CAKE I

5 egg whites
½ teaspoon cream tartar
1 cup sugar
4 tablespoons water

5 egg yolks
1 cup cake flour
Vanilla

1. Beat egg whites with cream of tartar until stiff. 2. Boil sugar and water until it threads. 3. Beat sugar syrup into egg whites and beat until cool. 4. Add the egg yolks beaten until thick. 5. Add cake flour sifted three times, and flavoring. 6. Bake in ungreased tin in cool oven, about 300°, for 45 minutes.

Mrs. William A. Judson.

SPONGE CAKE II

4 eggs
3 tablespoons cold water
1 cup sugar
1½ tablespoons cornstarch
Flour

1¼ teaspoons baking powder
¼ teaspoon salt
1 teaspoon lemon extract
1 teaspoon vanilla

1. Beat egg yolks and cold water. 2. Add sugar. 3. Measure cornstarch and fill cup with flour. Mix with baking powder and salt and add, mixing well. 4. Beat egg whites stiffly and add along with lemon and vanilla. 5. Bake in a slow oven (300°) about 1 hour.

Mrs. William E. Barth.

VELVET LUNCH CAKE

1 egg
1 cup butter
⅔ cup sugar
2 tablespoons molasses
1 cup raisins

1 teaspoon cinnamon
½ teaspoon cloves
1 teaspoon soda
1 cup sour milk
2 cups flour

1. Drop egg into mixing bowl and beat with dover beater. 2. Add sugar and beat some more. Then add molasses. 3. Melt butter and add to the above mixture. 4. Dissolve soda in sour milk. 5. Sift flour, cloves and cinnamon together. Add this alternately with the sour milk mixture. 6. Stir in the raisins. 7. Bake in two layers in a moderate oven, 350° to 375°. 8. Cool and ice with Seven Minute Icing.

Dorris Rounds

WHITE CAKE I

1½ cups sugar
½ cup butter
2½ cups flour

3 teaspoons baking powder
1 cup cold water
4 egg whites

1. Cream butter and sugar. 2. Sift flour before measuring, then add baking powder and sift five times. 3. Add flour mixture to butter and sugar alternately with cold water. 4. Add egg whites beaten into two ten-inch cake pans and bake at 375° for 20 minutes. 6. Put layers together with Seven Minute Icing and fresh cocoanut.

Edna Foss

WHITE CAKE II

½ cup shortening
1 cup sugar
¾ cup milk
2 cups flour
2 teaspoons baking powder

3 egg whites
½ teaspoon vanilla
½ teaspoon almond extract
Salt

1. Cream sugar and shortening together. 2. Sift flour, baking powder and salt together and add to above alternately with milk. 3. Beat egg whites until stiff and fold in. 4. Add vanilla and almond extract. 5. Bake in layer tins at 375°.

Grace S. Richmond

WHITE FRUIT CAKE

1 pound butter
1 pound fruit sugar
10 eggs
¾ cup orange juice
Juice of 1 lemon
4 tablespoons vanilla
5 cups flour

1 teaspoon baking powder
3 pounds white raisins
½ pound citron
½ pound lemon peel
½ pound orange peel
1 pound almonds, blanched
1 pound candied cherries

1. Cream butter and fruit sugar. 2. Add eggs two at a time and beat 3. Add orange juice, lemon juice and vanilla. 4. Sift flour and baking powder and add. 5. Add fruits and nuts and mix thoroughly. 6. Bake two hours in a slow oven, 300°.

The Late Mrs. Mabel Dixon

NOTE: So many of Mrs. Dixon's friends have enjoyed her White Fruit Cake recipe, they have requested that it be included in this group.

WHIPPED CREAM CAKE

2 eggs	1 teaspoon baking powder
1 cup sugar	½ cup boiling water
Vanilla	Whipped cream
1 cup flour	

1. Beat eggs and sugar until light. 2. Add boiling water and vanilla. 3. Sift flour and baking powder together and add. 4. Bake in slow oven 25 to 30 minutes. 5. Cover with thin coating of whipped cream.

Edna Foss

WONDER CAKE

4 egg yolks	Salt
7 tablespoons cold water	1 teaspoon vanilla
1½ cups sugar	4 egg whites
1½ cups flour	

1. Beat egg yolks. 2. Add water and beat 5 minutes. 3. Add sugar and beat 5 minutes. 4. Sift flour and salt together. Add and beat 5 minutes. 5. Add vanilla. 6. Beat egg whites until stiff and fold in above. 7. Bake 45 minutes in angel food tin in 300° oven.

Mrs. Carl Hoeppner

ICINGS and FILLINGS . . .

BUTTERSCOTCH ICING

1 cup brown sugar (firmly packed	¼ cup Spry or Crisco
2 tablespoons butter	¼ teaspoon salt
¼ cup milk	2 cups sifted confectioners' sugar
1 tablespoon light corn syrup	3 tablespoons hot milk

1. Combine brown sugar, butter, ¼ cup milk and corn syrup. 2. Cook until a small amount forms a hard ball in cold water. Stir while cooking. 3. Combine Spry or Criso and salt. 4. Add confectioners sugar, creaming well. 5. Add hot milk. 6. Pour this mixture gradually onto hot butterscotch mixture and beat until smooth and thick enough to spread.

Dorris Easling

CARAMEL SAUCE

½ pint heavy cream	2 cups brown sugar

1. Put sugar and cream over a slow fire and bring to a boil. 2. Remove at once and store in covered jars. This is excellent on sponge cake, ice cream and puddings.

Louise Emerson

CHOCOLATE ICING

1 cup sugar	1 teaspoon butter
½ cup milk	1 square chocolate (melted)
Yolk of 1 egg	

1. Mix all ingredients together. 2. Boil seven minutes. 3. Cool, then add 1 teaspoon vanilla, and beat.

Mrs. Harry Melin

CHOCOLATE WHIPPED CREAM ICING

¼ cup cocoa
⅓ cup confectioners' sugar
Hot water

1 teaspoon vanilla
½ pint cream, whipped

1. Mix cocoa and confectioners sugar. 2. Add hot water to make a stiff paste. 3. Add vanilla. 4. Whip ½ pint cream and add to the above.

Jeanette Tuohy

FILLING FOR GRAHAM CRACKERS

1 cup pulverized sugar
1 tablespoon (large) butter
2 tablespoons cocoa

2 tablespoons coffee
Graham crackers

1. Beat the sugar, butter, cocoa and coffee to a cream. 2. Spread between graham crackers.

Mrs. R. H. Watson.

MARSHMALLOW ICING

1. Follow above directions 2. After frosting becomes thick, add 8 marshmallows cut fine. Beat until marshmallows melt.

Frances H. Kerr.

NUT CARMEL FROSTING

1¼ cup brown sugar
¼ white sugar
½ nut meats

⅓ cup water
2 egg whites
1 teaspoon vanilla

1. Boil sugar and water to the long thread stage. 2. Beat egg whites stiffly. 3. Pour syrup gradually onto eggs, beating constantly. Continue beating until frosting is nearly cool. 4. Set pan containing mixture over hot water and cook, stirring constantly with a spoon until mixture becomes granular on the sides of the pan. 5. Remove from pan of hot water and beat, using a spoon, until mixture will hold its shape. 6. Add nut meats cut up and vanilla. 7. Spread quickly on cake.

Mrs. J. S. Stevenson.

PEAR AND FIG FILLING FOR CAKES AND COOKIES

2½ pounds pears
2½ pounds figs

2½ pounds sugar
1 pound raisins

1. Peel and quarter pears. 2. Grind pears, figs and raisins and add sugar. 3. Cook until thick. 4. Add juice of lemons to taste, if desired. 5. Put in jars and seal with parafin.

Mrs. E. W. Christoffers.

QUICK FLUFFY ICING

1 cup granulated sugar
Scant ½ cup boiling water

¼ teaspoon cream of tartar
1 egg white, unbeaten

1. Put sugar cream of tartar, and egg white into bowl, turn electric mixer to high speed and add boiling water gradually. 2. Beat for about 15 minutes or until smooth and thick.

Jean H. Sessions.

SEVEN MINUTE ICING

1 unbeaten egg white   3 tablespoons cold water
⅞ cup white sugar   ½ teaspoon vanilla

1. Place egg white, sugar and water in top of double boiler.   2. Place over boiling water and beat with electric beater for 7 minutes.   3. Add vanilla and mix well.   4. Spread on cake at once.

Louise Emerson.

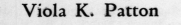

NOW READY FOR YOU . . . NEW AND BETTER

CHOCOLATE RECIPES!

SEND FOR OUR MAGNIFICENT NEW BOOK . . .

It's just off the press . . . Our magnificent new book of "Baker's Famous Chocolate Recipes"! Cost thousands of dollars to prepare! The most complete book of chocolate recipes ever written . . . 64 pages, 20 tempting color photographs, 143 recipes . . . The prize chocolate recipes of all times!

There are gorgeous cakes with luscious frostings, for those times when you serve just "refreshments." Delicate light cakes and small dessert ones, to follow a heavy meal. Simple but delicious every-day desserts, ranging all the way from a glorified bread pudding to a simply heavenly soufflé. And of course there are cookies, candies, frozen desserts, and beverages galore!

THIS HANDSOME BOOK WAS TWO YEARS IN PREPARATION . . . . IT IS YOURS FOR ONLY 10¢!

(Mail your request—See other side)

"Sample" Baker's Chocolate recipes from our new recipe book!

CHOCOLATE PEPPERMINT CAKE
(1 egg)

2 cups sifted Swans Down Cake Flour
1 teaspoon soda
½ teaspoon salt
⅓ cup butter or other shortening
1¼ cups sugar

1 egg, unbeaten
3 squares Baker's Unsweetened Chocolate, melted
1 teaspoon vanilla
½ cup thick sour cream

¾ cup sweet milk

Sift flour once, measure, add soda and salt, and sift together three times. Cream butter thoroughly, add sugar gradually, and cream together well. Add egg and beat very thoroughly; then chocolate and vanilla and blend. Add about ¼ of flour and beat well; then add sour cream and beat thoroughly. Add remaining flour, alternately with milk, beating after each addition until smooth. Turn into two greased 9-inch layer pans and bake in moderate oven (350° F.) 30 minutes, or until done. Spread Peppermint Frosting between layers and over cake. Decorate with a border of chocolate flakes. Double recipe for three 10-inch layers.

PEPPERMINT FROSTING

Combine 2 egg whites, 1½ cups sugar, 5 tablespoons water, and 1½ teaspoons corn syrup in top of double boiler, beating with rotary egg beater until thoroughly mixed. Place over rapidly boiling water, beat constantly with rotary egg beater, and cook 7 minutes, or until frosting will stand in peaks. Add bit of red coloring—only enough to tint a delicate pink. Remove from boiling water; flavor to taste with oil of peppermint (only a few drops are necessary). Beat until thick enough to spread. Spread on cake. While frosting is still soft, but cold, sprinkle chocolate flakes around top of cake to form 1-inch border.

For chocolate flakes, scrape Baker's Unsweetened Chocolate, holding knife at right angles to chocolate and scraping downward.

REGAL CHOCOLATE SAUCE

2 squares Baker's Unsweetened Chocolate
6 tablespoons water
½ cup sugar

Dash of salt
3 tablespoons butter
¼ teaspoon vanilla

Add chocolate to water and place over low flame, stirring until blended. Add sugar and salt and cook until sugar is dissolved and mixture very slightly thickened, stirring well. Add butter and vanilla. Makes 1 cup.

1978-A   Ptd. in U.S.A.

COOKIES . . .

ALL BRAN REFRIGERATOR COOKIES

½ cup shortening
½ cup sugar
½ cup molasses
½ cup All Bran
2 cups plus 1 tablespoon flour

1 egg
1½ teaspoons ginger
1½ teaspoons cinnamon
1½ teaspoons soda
¼ teaspoon salt

1. Cream shortening.   2. Add sugar, egg, molasses, All Bran. 3. Add sifted dry ingredients. 4. Form into rolls and store in refrigerator. 5. Slice into thin wafers so they will be crisp.   6. Bake at 400°.

Mrs. Harry A. King.

ALMOND COOKIES

1 cup butter
⅓ cup sugar
2 cups flour

1 teaspoon almond extract
1 egg
Chopped almonds

1. Mix butter, sugar, flour and almond extract.   2. Chill slighty.   3. Cut into squares.   4. Beat egg slightly and brush over tops of cookies.   5. Sprinkle with sugar and chopped almonds. 6. Bake at 400° until slightly brown.

Gladys S. Quist.

APPLE SAUCE COOKIES

1 egg
½ cup brown sugar
½ cup white sugar
½ cup shortening
  (use part butter)
1 cup sweetened apple sauce
1 teaspoon soda

1 tablespoon water
2¼ cups flour
1 teaspoon cinnamon
1 teaspoon nutmeg
1 teaspoon baking powder
1 cup chopped raisins

1. Beat egg well (not necessary to separate).   Beat in sugar and then beat some more.   3. Melt shortening and add.   4. Stir in the applesauce.   5. Dissolve the soda in water and add.   6. Sift flour, cinnamon, nutmeg and baking powder together and add a little at a time, beating well.   7. Mix in the raisins. 8. Drop by teaspoonfuls onto a greased cookies sheet.   9. Bake in a moderate oven, about 375°, for 15 minutes.

Carrie Slate.

BANANA COOKIES

1 cup brown sugar
1 egg
2 mashed bananas
½ cup butter
2 cups flour

1 teaspoon soda
½ teaspoon salt
1 teaspoon vanilla
½ cup walnut meats

1.Mix and beat in order given.   2. Drop from teaspoon onto greased cookie pans. 3. Bake about 10 minutes at 375°.

LeOra Weiss.

BOSTON FIG COOKIES

1 cup butter
1½ cups brown sugar
3 eggs
2½ cups flour
1 cup chopped walnuts

1 cup chopped figs
1 cup chopped dates
1 teaspoon soda
2 tablespoons hot water

1. Cream butter. 2. Add sugar and mix well. 3. Beat eggs and add. 4. Add sifted flour, walnuts, figs, dates and the soda dissolved in hot water. 5. Drop by teaspoonfuls on greased cookie sheet. 6. Bake in moderate oven, 350°.

Katherine Regan Kane, Dunkirk.

BROWN SUGAR COOKIES

2 cups brown sugar (well packed)
1 cup butter
2 eggs
1 cup hot water
1 teaspoon soda
1 teaspoon vanilla
¼ teaspoon salt
4½ cups flour
1½ teaspoons baking powder
1 cup chopped nuts

1. Cream butter and sugar. 2. Drop in eggs one at a time and mix well. 3. Dissolve soda in hot water and add. 4. Add vanilla, salt, flour and baking powder. 5. Add nuts if desired. 6. Chill in icebox. Roll out and sprinkle with sugar. 7. Bake at 400°.

Mrs. Carl Hoeppner, Dunkirk.

BUTTER FINGERS

⅞ cup butter
5 tablespoons sugar
1 egg
1 teaspoon vanilla
2 cups flour
1 cup ground pecans

1. Mix butter and sugar. 2. Add beaten egg, vanilla, flour and pecans. 3. Shape in small rolls the size of a finger and bake.

Mrs. Carl Brose, Minocqua, Wis.

BUTTERSCOTCH COOKIES

¼ cup shortening
1 cup brown sugar
1 teaspoon baking powder
¼ teaspoon salt
1 egg
1 cup flour
½ cup nuts, raisins or cocoanut

1. Cream sugar and shortening. 2. Add beaten eggs. 3. Sift salt, baking powder and flour and add. 4. Then add nuts and mix well. 5. Drop on buttered tins and bake at 400°.

Mrs. E. W. Christoffers.
Mrs. Cleveland Dietzen.

CARMEL SQUARES

⅓ cup melted butter
1 cup brown sugar
1 egg
1 cup cake flour sifted before measuring
1 teaspoon baking powder
Pinch of salt
1 teaspoon vanilla
½ cup walnut meats broken into small pieces

1. Mix in large bowl of electric mixer in the order given. 2. Bake in 350° oven for 25 minutes. 3. Cut in squares.

Louise Klopfer.

CHOCOLATE COOKIES I

2 squares chocolate
½ cup melted butter
1 cup sugar
½ cup flour
¼ teaspoon salt
2 well beaten eggs
½ cup chopped walnuts
1 teaspoon vanilla

1. Melt chocolate in double boiler. Remove from fire. 2. Add to this the melted butter. 3. Sift flour, sugar and salt together and add. 4. Stir in well beaten eggs. 5. Flavor with vanilla. 6. Spread with spatula on a greased cookie sheet until very thin. 7. Bake in an oven at about 400° for 10 minutes. 8. Cut into squares while warm and remove from pan immediately.

Mrs. William E. Barth.

CHOCOLATE COOKIES II

½ cup shortening
1 cup sugar
1 teaspoon salt
2 eggs
½ teaspoon soda

½ cup milk
3 squares chocolate
2½ cups flour
1 cup chopped nuts
1 teaspoon vanilla

1. Cream shortening and sugar. 2. Add well beaten eggs. 3. Sift salt, soda and flour together. 4. Add alternately with the milk. 5. Add melted chocolate, chopped nuts and vanilla. 6. Drop from spoon on buttered sheets. 7. Bake at 350°.

Mary E. Cook.

CHOCOLATE DROPS

1 pound bar Nestles Nut
. Chocolate

2 squares Bakers Chocolate
5 cups Corn Flakes

1. Melt chocolate over hot water. 2. Stir in corn flakes. 3. Drop from teaspoon onto wax paper and put in a cool place until hard.

Mrs. Robert Gardner.

CHOCOLATE JUMBLES

½ cup butter
1 cup brown sugar
½ cup sour cream
2 squares melted chocolate

1 egg
Salt
1½ cups flour
¼ cup nut meats

1. Cream butter and brown sugar. 2. Add remaining ingredients and mix well. 3. Drop from spoon. 4. Bake at 350°.

Frosting for Jumbles

1 egg
1 tablespoon sweet cream
1 square melted chocolate

½ cup powdered sugar
Vanilla

1. Beat egg and cream. 2. Add chocolate, sugar and vanilla. 3. Frost while jumbles are hot.

Mrs. Henry Fitzer.

CHOCOLATE MACAROONS

2 egg whites
1 cup sugar
¼ teaspoon salt

1½ squares chocolate
1½ cups shredded cocoanut
1 teaspoon vanilla

1. Beat egg whites until stiff. 2. Add sugar gradually, beating constantly. 3. Then add salt and melted chocolate. 4. Mix thoroughly and add cocoanut and vanilla. 5. Drop by spoonfuls on greased baking sheets. 6. Bake at 275° for about 30 minutes. — This makes about 1½ dozen macaroons.

Mary Howells.

CHOCOLATE SQUARES

2 ounces unsweetened chocolate (or 3 tablespoons cocoa)
½ cup butter
3 eggs

1 cup sugar
¾ cup flour
½ teaspoon baking powder
½ teaspoon salt

1.Put chocolate and butter over a low flame and blend. 2. Beat eggs until fluffy. 3. Add sugar, and the flour sifted with baking powder and salt. 4. To this add chocolate mixture last. 5. One cup nuts may be added, if desired 6. Bake for 20 minutes at 350°.

Jeanete Tuohy.

CINNAMON STARS (Christmas Cookies)

¾ cup shortening
1 cup brown sugar
2 eggs

¼ teaspoon salt
1 teaspoon baking powder
3 cups flour

1. Cream shortening and sugar together. 2. Beat eggs and add to above mixture. 3. Sift flour and measure 3 cups; add salt and baking powder and add to above. 4. Roll out thin; cut with star cookie cutter. 5. Bake in moderate oven until brown. 6. When cool, frost with ½ cup confectioners sugar and 2 tablespoons cinnamon.

Mrs. L. W. Foley, Dunkirk.

COCOANUT COOKIES

2 squares chocolate
1 can condensed milk

½ pound dry cocoanut

1.Melt chocolate in top of double boiler. 2. Add condensed milk. 3. Then add cocoanut. 4. Drop by teaspoonfuls on cookie sheet. 5. Bake in very slow oven (350°) about 10 minutes.

Mrs. Robert K. Pierce.

COCOANUT DREAM BARS

Part 1

¾ cup butter
⅓ cup light brown sugar

1½ cups flour

1. Cream butter and sugar together. 2. Add sifted flour and mix well. 3. Press evenly over the bottom of a nine-inch square pan. 4. Bake at 300° for 15 minutes until light brown. 5. Remove and cool.

Part 2

1½ cups brown sugar
2 eggs
1 cup cocoanut

2 tablepoons flour
¼ teaspoon baking powder
Sprinkle of salt

1. Beat eggs. 2. Add sugar, flour and baking powder which have been mixed together. 3. Add salt and cocoanut. Pour over first mixture and return to oven. 4. Bake until top is slightly browned. 5. Cool and cut in small squares.

Mrs. Harold F. Smith.

COOLIDGE COOKIES

1 cup butter (scant)
1½ cups sugar
3 cups sifted flour
½ teaspoon allspice
1 teaspoon cinnamon
1 cup dates

1 cup walnut meats
1 teaspoon baking powder
½ teaspoon salt
3 eggs
1 teaspoon soda in ½ cup
   hot water

1. Cream butter and sugar.   2. Add beaten eggs, and soda dissolved in hot water.
3. Sift flour, spices, baking powder and salt, and add.   4. Add dates and walnuts cut fine.   5. Roll to ⅛ inch thickness.   6. Bake at 385° about 10 minutes.

Rhea Stevens.

DATE BARS I

2 eggs
1 cup sugar
5 tablespoons hot water
1 cup flour
1 teaspoon baking powder

Salt
1 cup chopped nuts
1 package chopped dates
Vanilla

1. Beat eggs, add sugar and hot water.   2. Sift flour, baking powder and salt and add to mixture.   3. Then add nuts, dates and vanilla.   4. Bake in slow oven (325°). When cool cut in stripes and roll in powdered sugar.

Margaret Diers.

DATE BARS II

1 egg
1 cup sugar
½ cup milk
1 cup flour

2 teaspoons baking powder
½ teaspoon salt
1 cup dates
1 cup nuts

1. Beat egg, add sugar and mix well.   2. Sift flour, baking powder and salt and add alternately with milk.   3. Add chopped dates and nuts.   4. Bake in a shallow pan for 30 minutes in slow oven (about 325°).   5. Cut into bars and roll in powdered sugar.

Emma G. Hart.

DATE COOKIES

½ cup dates
1 teaspoon soda
⅓ cup boiling water
⅓ cup butter
1 cup light brown sugar

1 egg
⅓ cup chopped nuts
1¾ cups flour
2 teaspoons cream of tartar
½ teaspoon vanilla

1. Wash, stone and cut dates into pieces.   2. Sprinkle dates with soda and pour boiling water over them. Let stand until cool. 3. Cream, butter and sugar.
4. Add egg, the date mixture and chopped nuts.   4. Add flour sifted with cream of tartar.   6. Add vanilla last.   7. Drop by spoonfuls onto cookie sheet.
8. Bake at 350°.

Sarah Peters.

DATE SQUARES

1½ cups flour
1 cup brown sugar

¾ cup butter
1½ cup rolled oats

1. Mix above ingredients as for pie crust.   2. Put half of mixture in bottom of cake pan.   3. Make mixture of following ingredients and pour on this:

1 pound dates
1 cup boiling water

¾ cup sugar
½ lemon

1. Boil three minutes (until thick).   2. Add juice of 1-2 lemon.   3. Spread

on first mixture.   4. Put remaining half of first mixture on top.   5. Bake at 325° one half hour.

Mary Dunbar
Mrs. B. H. Ritenburg.

DROP COOKIES

2 cups light brown sugar
1 cup shortening (use part butter)
¼ teaspoon salt
2 eggs

¾ cup sour milk
1 teaspoon soda
4 cups flour
3 teaspoons baking powder
½ teaspoon nutmeg

1. Cream sugar and shortening.   2. Add beaten eggs.   3. Dissolve soda in sour milk and add.   4. Sift flour, salt, baking powder and nutmeg and add. 5. Drop from spoon and bake at 400°.

Josephine S. Brand.

DROP GINGER COOKIES

1 cup shortening
1 cup sugar
2 eggs
1 cup molasses
1 cup hot water

1 tablespoon soda
1 cup raisins
5 cups flour
1 tablespoon ginger
1 teaspoon salt

1. Cream shortening and sugar. 2. Add eggs and beat well. 3. Stir in molasses, then alternately the water in which soda has been dissolved, and the dry ingredients sifted together. 4. Add raisins and mix well. 5. Drop by spoonfuls onto greased baking pans. 6. Bake in a moderate oven (375°) about 15 minutes.

Eva Clark.

FRUIT COOKIES

½ cup shortening
⅓ cup sugar
1 egg
½ teaspoon salt
1 tablespoon orange juice

⅓ cup chopped dates
⅓ cup candied pineapple cut fine
1 cup flour
2 teaspoons baking powder

1. Cream shortening and sugar.   2. Add beaten egg.   3. Add orange juice and fruits.   4. Sift salt, flour and baking powder and add.   5. Drop from a spoon and bake at 350°.

Esther Rabin.

FUDGE SQUARES

3 tablespoons butter
1 cup sugar
1 egg
2 squares chocolate
1 teaspoon vanilla

⅓ cup milk
1 cup flour
1 teaspoon baking powder
½ teaspoon salt
½ cup chopped nutmeats

1. Cream butter and sugar. 2. Add beaten egg and melted chocolate. 3. Sift flour, baking powder and salt and add alternately with milk. 4. Add nuts and vanilla. 5. Bake in 8-inch square tin slowly (325°) 30 minutes.

Margaret Diers.

GRANDMA'S OLD FASHIONED GINGER COOKIES

1 cup sugar	2 eggs
1 cup butter	1 teaspoon ginger
1 cup black molasses	1 teaspoon cinnamon
2 teaspoons soda	3 cups flour
½ cup hot water	2 tablespoons vinegar
Salt	

1. Cream sugar and shortening.   2. Add molasses.   3. Dissolve soda in hot water and add. 4. Add eggs and stir well. 5. Sift cinnamon, ginger, salt and flour into mixture.   6. Roll cookies, cut, sprinkle with sugar.   7. Bake in a slow oven (325o).

Mrs. George Swift, Forestville.

GUM DROP COOKIES

4 eggs	2 cups flour
2 cups brown sugar	1 teaspoon baking powder
1 tablespoon cold milk	1 teaspoon cinnamon
½ pound gumdrops (1 cup)	

1. Beat eggs, add sugar and milk.   2. Sift flour, cinnamon and baking powder together and add.   3. Add gumdrops which have been cut into small pieces and rolled in flour.   4. Spread mixture thinly on a well-buttered cookie sheet. 5. Bake in a moderate oven (350o) until brown, — about 20 minutes.   6. Spread while hot with the following icing:—3 tablespoons melted butter, 1 cup powdered sugar, 1 1-2 tablespoon orange rind (grated) and orange juice.   7. Decorate with shredded cocoanut, candied cherries, nut meats or any other appropriate topping.   8. Cut into squares.   Makes about 30 large cookies.

Mrs. Henry Miller
Mrs. Robert K. Pierce.

GUM DROP SQUARES

2 eggs	10c nutmeats
1 cup brown sugar	5c fruit gumdrops
½ tablespoon cold water	1 cup flour

1. Beat eggs   2. Add sugar, water, nuts, fruit gumdrops and sifted flour. 3. Mix well and bake at 350o for 20 minutes.   4. Cut into squares.

Mrs. Gladys S. Quist.

ICE BOX COOKIES

2 eggs	1 teaspoon soda
1 cup white sugar	5 teaspoons hot water
1 cup light brown sugar	2 teaspoons vanilla
1 pound shortening	5 cups flour
1 teaspoon salt	2 cups nut meats

1. Cream shortening, sugar and eggs.   2. Add salt, hot water in which soda has been dissolved, flour and nuts, — then the vanilla.   3. Let stand 20 to 30 minutes. Form into two rolls and let stand in refrigerator over night.   4. Slice very thin and bake in a moderate oven—350o as wanted.

Dorothy Sievert.

MINCE MEAT COOKIES

1 cup butter
1½ cups sugar
3 eggs
1 teaspoon soda

1½ tablespoons hot water
3¼ cups flour
1 small package mincemeat
½ teaspoon salt

1. Cream butter and add sugar gradually. 2. Add eggs well beaten. 3. Add soda dissolved in hot water and half the flour mixed and sifted with salt. 4. Add mince meat broken into small pieces, and the remainder of the flour. Nutmeats may be added, if desired. 5. Drop by spoonfuls an inch apart on a greased baking sheet. 6. Bake at 350° until golden brown. 7. Remove from oven when still soft and cover before entirely cool.

Frances H. Kerr.

MOLASSES BROWNIES

⅔ cup shortening
⅔ cup brown sugar
4 eggs
⅔ cup molasses

2 cups flour
2 cups walnuts
½ teaspoon salt

1. Cream shortening: add sugar gradually. 2. Add beaten eggs, molasses, flour and salt and the walnuts. 3. Bake in a shallow pan in moderate oven (350°). 4. Cut into squares or bars.

Mrs. S. E. Mead.

MOLASSES REFRIGERATOR COOKIES

1 cup shortening
2 cups brown sugar
¾ cup molasses
2 eggs
3½ cups flour

1 teaspoon baking powder
1 teaspoon cinnamon
1 teaspoon ginger
½ teaspoon salt

1. Mix shortening and sugar. 2. Add molasses, and beaten eggs. 3. Sift flour, baking powder, spices and salt. 4. Mix well, put in refrigerator and freeze hard. 5. Cut very thin, and bake in quick oven (425°).

Marguerite Taft.

NEWTON COOKIES

½ cup butter
1 cup sugar
1 egg
½ cup sweet milk

1 teaspoon soda
4 cups flour
2 teaspoons cream of tartar
1 teaspoon vanilla

1. Cream butter and sugar. 2. Add beaten egg. 3. Sift dry ingredients and add alternately with milk. 4. Add vanilla. 5. Roll and cut and put together with filling.

Filling for Newton Cookies

½ cup sugar
Pinch salt
1 cup chopped raisins

1 tablespoon flour
½ cup water
Juice ½ lemon

1. Mix sugar, flour and salt together. 2. Add water, raisins and lemon juice. 3. Cook until thick. 4. Bake cookies at 400°, 12 to 15 minutes

Louise Klopfer.

NUT SQUARES

1 cup brown sugar	3 tablespoons flour
1 egg (beaten)	2 cups nutmeats

1. Mix above ingredients well. 2. Bake at 350º in well-buttered and well-floured tins. 3. Makes 16 squares.

Clara Wheelock.

OATMEAL CRISP COOKIES

1 cup sugar	1 teaspoon soda
½ cup shortening (melted)	3 tablespoons molasses
1 egg	1½ cups oatmeal (uncooked)
½ teaspoon salt	1½ cups flour

1. Cream sugar and shortening. 2. Add beaten egg. 2. Sift salt and flour and add. 4. Dissolve soda in molasses and add. 5. Add oatmeal, mixing thoroughly. The batter is very thick. 6. Drop on greased cookies pans, pressing each cookie flat with bottom of water humbler. 7. Bake in moderate oven. 8. Cinnamon and raisins may be added, if desired. Makes about 2 dozen cookies.

Mrs. S. E. Mead.

OATMEAL DROP COOKIES

1 cup brown sugar	1 teaspoon cinnamon
1 cup shortening	4 tablespoons boiling water
2 cups flour	1 cup nuts
1 teaspoon baking powder	1 teaspoon soda
2 eggs (beaten)	1 cup raisins
2 cups oatmeal	

1. Cream shortening and add sugar. 2. Add beaten eggs and soda dissolved in hot water. 3. Sift flour, baking powder and cinnamon and add. 4. Add oatmeal, nuts and raisins and mix well. 5. Drop on buttered pans and bake at 350º.

Mrs. Clyde Brumm.

OATMEAL FILLED COOKIES
Filling

Make filling as follows and let cool while mixing dough:

1 cup pitted dates, cut in small pieces	½ cup brown or white sugar
1¾ cups drained, cooked apricots, unsweetened	2 tablespoons liquid from apricots

1. Blend fruit and sugar in sauce pan. 2. Boil until mixture thickens —about 3 minutes. — Canned peaches may be substituted for the apricots.

Dough

¾ cup melted shortening (use half butter)	1 teaspoon soda
1 cup brown sugar	2 cups quick cooking oatmeal
2 cups flour	1 teaspoon vanilla

1. Blend shortening with sugar. 2. Sift flour once before measuring, then sift flour and soda together and mix with oatmeal. 3. Blend dry mixture and vanilla

with sugar shortening. 4. Work into dough with hands. 5. Spread in well-greased 8x12 pan (using half the mixture). 6. Spread with filling and top with remaining dough. Press down. 7. Bake at 350° for 30 minutes.

Mrs. Henry Miller.

OATMEAL LACE COOKIES

3 cups oatmeal
3 teaspoons baking powder
1 cup sugar
¼ cup butter
2 eggs
Salt

1. Mix together sugar and butter. 2. Add beaten eggs, baking powder, salt and oatmeal. 3. Mix thoroughly and drop by spoonfuls on well greased tins. 4. Bake in moderate oven — 350°.

Mrs. E. W. Christoffers.

ORANGE COOKIES

1 cup sugar
¾ cup shortening
Grated rind of 1 orange
2 eggs, beaten
3 cups flour
4 teaspoons baking powder
½ teaspoon salt
½ cup orange juice

1. Cream sugar, shortening and orange rind. 2. Add well-beaten eggs. 3. Sift flour, baking powder and salt and add alternately with orange juice. 4. Chill several hours in ice box before rolling out. 5. Bake at 400°.

Mrs. M. B. Douthett.

PEANUT BUTTER COOKIES

2 cups brown sugar
½ cup shortening
½ cup peanut butter
2 beaten eggs
1 teaspoon soda
½ teaspoon salt
2 to 3 cups flour
Vanilla

1. Cream shortening and brown sugar. 2. Add peanut butter and beaten eggs. 3. Sift soda, salt and flour and add. 4. Add vanilla, mix well, and knead into roll with hands. 5. Place in ice box over night. 6. Bake at 350°.

Ellen Akins.

PEANUT BUTTER DROP COOKIES

½ cup butter or other shortening
1½ cups brown sugar
10 tablespoons peanut butter
1¾ cups flour
1 teaspoon baking powder
½ teaspoon salt
½ cup milk or more
Vanilla

1. Cream the shortening, add the sugar and then the peanut butter. Mix well. 2. Add the beaten eggs and vanilla. 3. Add the dry ingredients sifted together, alternately with the milk. 4. Drop by spoonfuls on greased pan. Sprinkle with nuts if desired. Bake about 20 minutes in a moderate oven.

Mrs. Albert Piehl.

PFEFFERNUESSE (GERMAN CHRISTMAS COOKIE)

1 pound granulated sugar
4 eggs
1 teaspoon baking powder
1 teaspoon nutmeg
1 teaspoon cinnamon
1 teaspoon cloves
4 cups flour

1. Cream sugar and eggs.   2. Add baking powder and spices.   3. Mix in the flour. The mixture must be stiff enough to roll and cut with a thimble.   4. Let stand all night and in the morning turn upside down on pan.   5. Bake until light brown at 350°.

Mrs. L. W. Foley.

PENUCHE BARS

¼ cup shortening
1 cup brown sugar
2 eggs
1 teaspoon vanilla

¾ cup cake flour
½ teaspoon salt
1 cup chopped walnuts

1. Cream shortening and sugar.   2. Add the eggs, well beaten, and the vanilla. 3. Sift the dry ingredients together and stir in the nuts.   Combine with first mixture.   4. Bake in shallow, oiled pan(batter ¼ inch thick) at 375°.   5. When cool, cut into bars.

Mrs. S. E. Mead.

PERFECT BROWNIES

¼ cup butter
1 cup sugar
2 eggs, slightly beaten
¼ cup milk
⅔ cup pastry flour

⅓ teaspoon salt
½ cup nuts, chopped
½ teaspoon vanilla
2½ squares chocolate

1. Cream the butter.   Add sugar and cream again.   2. Add the eggs.   3. Add flour (to which salt has been added) alternately with milk, beginning and end with flour.   4. Add nuts, vanilla and melted chocolate.   5. Pour into a shallow pan and bake at 350° for 15 minutes, or until done.

Mrs. Harold F. Smith.

PINEAPPLE DROP COOKIES

1 cup butter
1 cup brown sugar
1 cup white sugar
2 eggs
1 cup crushed pineapple,
    drained

4 cups flour
2 teaspoons baking powder
½ teaspoon salt
½ teaspoon soda
Nuts, if desired

1. Cream butter and sugar.   2. Add well-beaten eggs and   pineapple.   3. Sift flour, baking powder, salt and soda together   and   add,   mixing   thoroughly. 4. Bake at 375°.   This receipe makes 100 small cookies.

Mrs. Robert Ross.
Mrs. Robert D. Sprague.

PINWHEEL COOKIES

½ cup butter
½ cup sugar
1 egg
3 tablespoons milk

1½ cups flour
⅛ teaspoon salt
½ teaspoon baking powder

1. Cream butter and sugar thoroughly. 2. Add egg well beaten. 3. Sift dry ingredients and add alternately with milk. 4. Divide dough into two parts. 5. Add

1 square melted chocolate to one part, or tint with food coloring. 6. Roll both parts out to about ¼ inch thickness. 7. Place one part on top of the other and roll thin. 8. Then roll like jelly roll and chill in ice box for several hours. 9. Slice and bake in quick oven, about 400°.

Mrs. Robert D. Sprague.

PUMPKIN COOKIES

1¼ cups brown sugar
½ cup shortening
2 eggs, well beaten
1½ cups canned pumpkin
1 teaspoon vanilla
½ teaspoon salt (heaping)
¼ teaspoon ginger

½ teaspoon nutmeg
½ teaspoon cinnamon
1 teaspoon orange extract
2½ cups flour
4 teaspoons baking powder
1 cup raisins
1 cup chopped nuts

1. Cream sugar and shortening. 2. Add eggs, pumpkin and seasonings. 3. Add sifted flour and baking powder, and the fruit and nuts. 4. Drop by teaspoonfuls on well greased baking sheet. 5. Bake at 400° for 15 minutes.

Gladys M. Parker.

REFRIGERATOR COOKIES

1 cup soft butter
2 cups dark brown sugar
(contents of 1 lb. box)
2 beaten eggs
4 cups flour (sifted before measuring)

1 teaspoon baking powder
1 teaspoon soda
2 cups walnuts broken into pieces
1 teaspoon vanilla

1. Cream butter and sugar. 2. Add beaten eggs, flour sifted with baking powder and soda, nuts and vanilla. 3. Roll into a loaf and let stand in refrigerator over night. 4. Cut in thin slices and bake in a moderate oven 350°.

Margaret Gregory.

SCOTCH COOKIES

1 pound butter
8 ounces ground blanched almonds
½ cup sugar

4 cups flour
1 teaspoon vanilla
1 teaspoon lemon

1. Cream butter and sugar. 2. Add flour, almonds and extracts. 3. Roll into small balls and shape into half-moons. 4. Bake in 400° oven for 15 or 20 minutes.

Mrs. J. C. Boody.

SHORTBREAD

1 pound butter
2 cups brown sugar

4 cups flour

1. Cream the butter with the sugar. 2. Sift the flour and add until the mixture becomes a firm paste. 3. Knead well on a wooden board and pat into a dough about ½ to ¾ inch thick. 4. Cut into squares and bake in moderate oven.

Lenore Breeler.

SOFT GINGER COOKIES

1 cup brown sugar	2 teaspoons ginger
1 cup shortening	1 teaspoon cinnamon
1 cup sour milk	1 teaspoon vanilla
1½ cups New Orleans molasses	1 rounding teaspoon soda
2 eggs	4½ cups flour
1 teaspoon salt	½ teaspoon cream of tartar

1. Cream sugar and shortening. 2. Add sour milk, molasses and beaten eggs. 3. Dissolve soda in a little hot water and add. 4. Sift salt, spices. flour and cream of tartar and add. 5. Add vanilla, mix well and let stand in refrigerator over night. 6. In morning, roll out and bake in 375º oven.

Grace S. Richmond.

SOFT SUGAR COOKIES

1½ cups sugar	1 cup sour milk
1 cup butter	1 teaspoon soda
Salt	3½ cups flour
1 teaspoon baking powder	1 teaspoon vanilla
2 eggs	

1. Cream butter and sugar. 2. Add beaten eggs, and soda dissolved in sour milk. 3. Sift salt, baking powder and flour and add. 4. Add vanilla and mix well. 5. Roll and cut on floured board. 6. Bake at 400º.

Edna Foss, Dunkirk.

SOUR CREAM COOKIES

1 cup thick sour cream	½ teaspoon salt
1 teaspoon soda	½ teaspoon nutmeg or mace
1 cup sugar	Vanilla
2 eggs	Scant 2½ cups flour

1. Cream sugar and beaten eggs. 2. Dissolve soda in cream and add. 3. Sift flour, salt and nutmeg and add. 4. Add vanilla and mix well. 5. Drop from spoon, or roll with as little flour as possible. 6. Sprinkle sugar on top and bake at 350º to 375º.
Note: Always use same amount of sugar as cream. If shortage of cream, use ½ cup cream and scant ½ cup butter.

Lotta L. Deane.

SOUR CREAM REFRIGERATOR COOKIES

1½ cups butter	1 teaspoon baking powder
1¼ cups brown sugar	3½ cups flour
½ cup sour whipping cream	1 teaspoon vanilla
½ teaspoon soda	

1. Cream butter and add sugar gradually. 2. Stir soda with whipping cream and add. 3. Sift baking powder with flour and add. 4. Add vanilla, roll into loaf and leave in refrigerator over night. 5. Cut in thin slices, place one blanched almond in center of each cookie and sprinkle with crushed loaf sugar. 6. Bake in slow oven — 325º.

Margaret Gregory.

SUGAR COOKIES

1 cup light brown sugar
½ cup butter
1 egg
½ cup buttermilk

½ teaspoon soda
1 teaspoon baking powder
Flour

1. Cream butter and brown sugar.   2. Add beaten egg.   3. Disolve soda in buttermilk and add.   4. Add baking powder and flour enough to make a dough stiff enough to roll out.   5. Bake at 400°.

Elizabeth Stevens
Anna G. Hall.

SUGAR COOKIES II

2½ cups sifted pastry flour
2 teaspoons baking powder
½ teaspoon nutmeg
Grated rind of lemon

1 cup sugar
½ cup butter
1 tablespoon cream
2 egg yolks

1. Cream butter and sugar.   2. Add well-beaten egg yolks, lemon rind and cream.
3. Sift flour, nutmeg and baking powder and add.   4. Roll on floured board, cut and bake at 400°.

Mary Howells.

TOFFEE SQUARES

1 cup butter
1 cup sugar
1 egg
2 cups flour

1 tablespoon cinnamon
1½ cups nuts chopped very fine
Few grains salt

1. Cream sugar and shortening. 2. Add egg yolk, salt, flour and cinnamon. 3. Place in long cookie tin, already floured, spreading evenly not over ¼ inch thick.
4. Over surface pour egg white slightly beaten and cover with nuts.   5. Bake five minutes at 375° and fifteen to twenty minutes at 400°.

Norinne Walker.

WAYVE'S AFTER SCHOOL COOKIES

1 cup seedless raisins
¾ cup hot water
1 teaspoon soda
½ cup butter
½ teaspoon salt
½ teaspoon cinnamon

1¼ cups brown sugar
1 egg
2 cups flour
1 teaspoon baking powder
½ cup chopped nut meats

1. Grind the raisins. 2. Put soda in hot water and pour over raisins. Cool.
3. Cream sugar and butter, and add beaten egg. 4. Sift cinnamon, baking powder, salt and flour slowly into mixture. 5. Drop by teaspoonfuls onto greased pan. 6. Bake at 350° for 15 minutes. — These cookies are good for after school—one night only — if your children have friends.

Mrs. Otis J. Swift.

DOUGHNUTS . . .

MY MOTHER'S FRIED CAKES

1 cup sugar
1 egg
3 tablespoons melted lard
1 cup sweet milk

1 teaspoon salt
3 teaspoons baking powder
⅛ teaspoon soda
Flour

1. Mix sugar, beaten egg and melted lard. 2. Add milk alternately with salt, baking powder, soda and flour enough to mix rather stiff. 3. Fry in hot lard. The lard should be hot enough to brown a cube of bread in 60 seconds.

Thelma Green.

POTATO DOUGHNUTS

1 cup hot mashed potatoes
1 cup sugar
2 tablespoons shortening
½ teaspoon salt
1 teaspoon nutmeg

3 teaspoons baking powder
1 cup sweet milk
2 eggs, lightly beaten
Flour enough to roll,
about 4 cups

1. Add sugar, and shortening to hot mashed potatoes. Mix. 2. Add vanilla and dry ingredients. 3. Add flour alternately with milk, then add beaten eggs. 4. Roll on well-floured board to ¼inch thickness. Cut. 5. Fry in deep fat.

Virginia Morrison.

TEA DOUGHNUTS

½ cup sugar
2 eggs
⅓ cup cream
2½ cups cake flour

Grating of nutmeg
4 teaspoons baking powder
¼ teaspoon salt

1. Beat eggs until light. 2. Add sugar gradually, beating all the while; then add cream. 3. Sift flour, baking powder, salt and nutmeg together twice and combine with first mixture.   This should make a fairly soft dough. Add a little more cream or milk if too stiff.   4. Roll out lightly and quickly on a floured board to ¼ inch thickness. 5. Cut with small round cutter and fry at once in deep, hot fat. 6. Drain on unglazed paper and sprinkle with powdered sugar.

Gladys M. Parker.

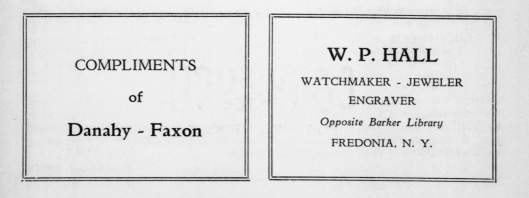

DESSERTS . . .

FROZEN DESSERTS - ICES . . .

AVACADO ICE
2 cups mashed Avocado pear   Juice of 1½ lemons
1 cup sugar

Combine the mashed avacado, sugar and the lemon juice and mix thoroughly. Put in freezing tray and stir occasionally. May be used as a dessert or as an accompaniment to the meat course.

Faye Burrows.

BANANA ICE
1 mashed banana   1 lemon — juice and pulp
¾ cup sugar   1 cup milk
1 orange — juice and pulp

Mix the sugar with the fruit juices. Add the milk. Freeze.

Mary Dunbar.

RASPBERRY ICE
1 quart water   ¾ can crushed raspberries or
1½ cups sugar   1 pint of fresh raspberries
Juice of 1 lemon   stewed with ¼ cup sugar
½ package raspberry Jello

Boil the sugar and water slowly for 10 minutes. Pour over the Jello and cool. Add the raspberries which have been put through a course stainer. When cool, add the lemon juice and freeze.

Mrs. Harry A. King.

ICE CREAMS . . .

VANILLA ICE CREAM I (Basic recipe)
3 cups milk   2 tablespoons vanilla
3 tablespoons flour   ½ pint whipping cream
¾ cup sugar

1. Place milk in the double boiler. Bring to a boil. 2. Mix the flour and sugar and add to the milk. Cook 10 minutes. 3. Remove from the fire, stirring occasionally to prevent skin forming on top while cooling. 4. Add vanilla. 5. Place in refrigerator tray and when it begins to freeze stir thoroughly. Allow to become partially frozen, then add cream which has been whipped. Stir once or twice before thoroughly frozen.
This recipe may be easily varied. See below:

Lemon Ice Cream
To Vanilla Ice Cream add the juice of 4 lemons before adding the whipped cream and after the custard has begun to freeze. Omit the vanilla. Add the whipped cream.

Pineapple Ice Cream
To vanilla Ice Cream add two small cans of crushed pineapple, drained, the juice of two lemons after the custard has begun to freeze. Omit vanilla. Add the whipped cream.

Grape Ice Cream

Boil two quarts of blue grapes for 3 minutes, strain and cool. Add to Vanilla Ice Cream custard when it has begun to freeze. Juice of 1 lemon may be added. Omit Vanilla. Add whipped cream.

Apricot Ice Cream

Prepare 2 cups apricot pulp, either by stewing dried fruit or straining canned fruit. Add to custard while freezing. Juice of 1 lemon if desired. Omit vanilla. Add whipped cream.

Peach Ice Cream

Prepare 2 cups of peach pulp, either fresh or canned. Add to custard while freezing. Omit vanilla. Add whipped cream.

Strawberry Ice Cream

Prepare 2 cups of strawberry pulp, either fresh or canned, or 1½ cups of strawberry jam. Add to custard while freezing. Omit vanilla. Add whipped cream.

Elizabeth Wells.

VANILLA ICE CREAM II

1 cup milk	4 eggs
⅓ cup sugar	Salt
12 marshmallows	Vanilla
1 tablespoon butter	½ pint whipping cream

1. Heat the milk and sugar. Add the marshmallows, butter, salt and vanilla. 2. Pour this mixture over the beaten egg yolks and cook in double boiler until it thickens. Cool. 3. Add the beaten egg whites and the cream which has been whipped. Freeze.

Mrs. Emmet Ross, Jamestown, N. Y.

ICE CREAM (Made in old fashioned freezer)

1 quart milk	1 tablespoon flour
1 pint cream	Salt
1 cup sugar	Flavoring
3 eggs	

1. Scald the milk. 2. Beat the eggs well and add the sugar and flour to this. 2. Then pour the hot milk over this. 3. Cook the mixture, preferably over water until you are sure it no longer tastes of flour. Cool. 4. Add salt and flavoring. Remember that sweetness and flavoring are apt to freeze out somewhat.

Thelma Green.

CRANBERRY FRAPPE

1½ teaspoons gelatine (Knox's)	½ cup cold water
1 pint cranberries	1½ cups boiling water
1¼ cups sugar	1½ tablespoons lemon juice

1. Cook the cranberries and put through a sieve. 2. Soften gelatine in cold water and add to the cranberries. 3. Add the sugar and lemon juice, stir until sugar is dissolved. 4. Chill and freeze.

Mrs. Robert K. Pierce.

FIVE THREES

3 bananas	3 cups sugar
3 lemons	3 cups water
3 oranges	

1. Mash bananas to a paste. Blend with the sugar. 2. Add juices and pulp of the fruit and add water. 3. Freeze in refrigerator, stirring two or three times at half-hour intervals.

Margaret Gailewicz.

MAPLE PARFAIT
4 eggs
1 cup hot maple syrup

1 pint thick cream

1. Beat egg yolks and add the syrup slowly. Cook until thick. Cool. 2. Add the cream and beaten egg whites. 3. Freeze at the coldest point. Stir once before freezing.

Mrs. Clyde Brumm.

SHERBETS . . .
APRICOT SHERBET
2 eggs
1 cup sugar
1 cup apricots, after cooked
and strained

Juice of 2 lemons
Grated rind of 1 lemon
1 quart milk

1. Beat egg yolks until light and add sugar, apricots, lemon juice, lemon rind and milk. 2. Put in freezing tray and add beaten egg whites after the mixture has started to freeze.

Mrs. F. E. Brockett.

LEMON SHERBET
3 cups sugar
3 pints milk

Grated rind of 1 lemon
¼ cup lemon juice

1. Scald sugar, milk and lemon rind. Cool. 2. Partly freeze and add lemon juice and finish freezing.

Mrs. F. E. Brockett.

LEMON AND ORANGE SHERBET
Juice and rind of 1 orange
Juice and rind of 1 lemon
1½ cups sugar
2 cups condensed milk

1 cup sweet milk
¼ teaspoon salt
1 tablespoon gelatine

1. Dissolve the gelatine in a little milk set in hot water. Add juice of fruit and grated rind to sugar and combine all ingredients. 2. Turn into freezing tray. Stir twice during freezing. Freeze rapidly for smooth mixture.

Mrs. Marcus Morrison.

ORANGE SHERBET
¾ cup sugar
¾ cup water
Grated rind of 1 orange
1¾ cups orange juice

Juice of 1 lemon
¾ cup cream
2 egg whites
1 cup whipping cream

1. Cook water, orange rind and sugar slowly for 5 minutes. Strain and cool.
2. Add to fruit juices. 3. Pour into refrigerator tray and freeze until quite firm.

4. Remove and beat with rotary beater until light. Stir in ¾ cup cream and fold in egg whites stiffly beaten and to which has been added a pinch of salt. 5. Return to tray and stir 2 or 3 times while freezing. 6. Before entirely frozen whip 1 cup cream, slightly sweetened, and pour over the top. Finish freezing.

Margaret Gregory.

SHERBET

1 cup orange juice	1 teaspoon lemon or orange
½ cup lemon juice	rind
1¼ cups sugar	1 pint milk

Mix and dissolve the fruit juices and sugar. Add the milk and freeze.

Mrs. Harry Melin.

PIES . . .

ALABAMA PECAN PIE

½ cup sugar	1 teaspoon vanilla
1 tablespoon flour	1 cup white cooking syrup
½ cup butter	1 cup broken pecans
2 eggs	

1. Mix sugar and flour, add butter and work until creamy. 2. Add eggs and beat with rotary beater until smooth. 3. Add vanilla and syrup and continue beating. 4. Stir in pecans. 5. Pour into a pastry shell which has been placed in a hot oven (450°) for 3 minutes or until slightly browned. 6. After pecan filling has been added reduce oven temperature to 325° and continue baking until center is firm to the touch. — Cinnamon, nutmeg and any desired spices may be substituted for the vanilla.

Mrs. Daniel Harmon.

CARAMEL PIE

1 cup brown sugar	1 heaping tablespoon corn-
Butter size of an egg	starch
1½ cups milk	2 eggs

1. Melt sugar and butter together in double boiler and add milk. 2. Mix cornstarch with little milk and add to mixture and cook until thick. 3. Add yolks of eggs and pour into baked pie shell. 4. Beat whites of eggs and use for top of pie.

Mary Howells.

CHERRY PIE AND PASTRY

2½ cups canned cherries	1 cup sugar
2½ tablespoons tapioca	⅛ teaspoon salt
½ cup cherry juice	1 teaspoon butter

1. Mix the juice with the sugar, tapioca and salt and let stand while making the pastry. 2. Mix the cherries with the melted butter and with above mixture. 3. Pour into crust and bake at 400° for 10 minutes, then reduce heat to 350° and bake for 20 minutes.

Pastry

1½ cups flour	1 tablespoon salt
½ cup shortening, lard or	2 or 3 tablespoons milk
Crisco	

Blend the lard or other shortening, flour and salt and add milk. Roll out and line pie tin, reserving half for the top.

Mrs. L. H. Bittner.

CHOCOLATE CHIFFON PIE

2 tablespoons melted bitter chocolate
½ cup boiling water
1 cup sugar
1 envelope Knox's gelatine
⅓ cup cold water

4 egg yolks, beaten
½ teaspoon salt
1 teaspoon vanilla
4 egg whites beaten with
½ cup sugar

1. Pour boiling water over melted chocolate. 2. Add ½ cup sugar and gelatine which has been dissolved in cold water. 3. Add beaten egg yolks, salt and vanilla. Do not cook. 4. Beat the egg whites stiff, add remaining ½ cup sugar and fold into chocolate mixture. 5. Pour into baked pie crust. 6. Place in refrigerator until set. 7. Cover with whipped cream and serve.

Mrs. E. M. Bowen.

COCOANUT CUSTARD PIE

3 eggs slightly beaten
⅛ teaspoon salt
½ cup sugar

3 cups scalded milk
1 cup cocoanut

1. Line a pie tin with pastry. 2. Combine eggs, salt and sugar. 3. Add milk gradually, then cocoanut. 4. Bake in hot oven 400° for 15 minutes, then decrease heat to 350° for 30 minutes.

Mrs. J. C. Boody.

CONCORD GRAPE PIE

5 cups stemmed grapes
1 cup canned pineapple, sliced, cut in small pieces
1½ cups sugar

3 tablespoons cornstarch
¾ teaspoon salt
Baked pastry shell

1. Wash grapes and slip skins from pulp. 2. Boil pulp 3 minutes, rub through sieve to remove seeds. 3. Combine cornstarch, sugar, salt, and grape pulp. Cook until thickened, stirring constantly. 4. With scissors cut grape skins fine. 5. Add to mixture together with pineapple. 6. Pour into pastry-lined pie plate. Cover with strips of pastry lattice fashion. 7. Bake in moderate oven, 350° F. for 10 minutes. Serve cool. Makes a 9-inch pie.

Louise S. Butler.

GRAHAM CRACKER PIE

18 graham crackers rolled fine
½ cup melted butter

½ cup sugar

Mix the sugar and butter with the graham cracker crumbs and pat into a pie tin. Reserve 1 cup of the crumbs for the top. Place in the icebox to chill while you prepare the filling.

Custard Filling:

3 eggs
4 heaping teaspoons cornstarch

2 cups milk
½ cup sugar
Flavoring

1. Beat the egg yolks and combine with the rest of the ingredients. 2. Cook in the double boiler until thick. 3. Pour into the crumb crust. 4. Top with meringue made from the egg whites beaten stiffly. Sprinkle the remaining crumbs on top. Brown in oven.

Virginia Berkwater.

GRAPE JUICE PIE

2 cups grape juice
3 tablespoons corn-starch
6 tablespoons sugar

½ teaspoon salt
1 egg or 2 egg yolks, beaten
1 tablespoon lemon juice

1. Add the lemon juice last and cook in double boiler until thick. 2. Cool slightly. 3. Pour into baked pie crust. 4. Top with whipped cream.

Mrs. Louise L. Phillips.

GRAPE PIE

1½ cups grape skins and pulp
    of grapes
2 level tablespoons flour

½ to ¾ cup sugar
1 egg yolk

1. Skin grapes. 2. Cook pulp over low flame five minutes, then strain over grape skins. 3. Add sugar, flour, and yolk of egg. 4. Line a pie tin with rich pastry and pour in mixture and bake in moderate oven about 45 minutes. 5. Top pie with meringue or whipped cream.

Mrs. Raymond W. Foley.

LEMON CHIFFON PIE

4 eggs
1 cup sugar
Juice of 1 lemon

1 teaspoon gelatine in ⅓ cup
    cold water
Baked pie shell
Whipped cream

1. Cook egg yolks, ½ cup sugar and juice of lemon in double boiler until thick. 2. Stir in gelatine, which has been placed in water, in mixture.3. Beat whites of the 4 eggs, add remaining ½ cup sugar and slowly stir into above mixture. 4. Put in baked pie shell and serve with whipped cream flavored slightly with vanilla and sugar.

Mrs. E. W. Christoffers.

LEMON SPONGE PIE

2 tablespoons butter (large)
1 cup sugar
3 egg yolks, beaten
1 rounded tablespoon flour

1 cup milk
1 lemon, juice and grated rind
3 egg whites, beaten stiff

1. Cream butter, egg yolks, sugar, and flour. 2. Add milk, a little at a time, and lemon. 3. Fold in egg whites. 4. Place in unbaked pie shell and bake slowly 30 to 45 minutes. 5. Serve with whipped cream if desired.

Evelyn C. Fairbanks.

LEMON PIE

1 cup sugar
2 tablespoons cornstarch
Juice of one lemon

1½ cups hot water
2 eggs
Pie shell

1. Combine sugar with cornstarch and add juice of lemon, yolks of eggs, and water. Cook in double boiler until mixture thickens. 2. Pour into baked pie shell and use whites of eggs for meringue. 3. Bake in slow oven long enough to brown meringue.

Meringue
1. Add 2 tablespoons cold water to egg whites and beat until stiff. 2. Add 2 tablespoons sugar to the beaten whites and top pie.

Mrs. Edward N. Button.

MINCEMEAT PIE

1 package mincemeat
2 cups hot water
1 cup raisins

2 large apples, chopped
1 cup maple syrup
Lump butter

1. Add hot water to mincemeat, then combine with other ingredients. 2. Cook mixture slowly until apples are tender. 3. Bake in oven 375º for 30 minutes. This makes two pies.

Mrs. Amos E. Hall.

PASTRY SHELLS

½ cup lard
1 cup boiling water
1 cup flour

4 eggs
½ teaspoon salt

1. Boil lard, water, salt, and flour. Stir. 2. Remove from fire, add one egg at a time. 3. Bake 30 minutes in hot oven.

Mrs. Harry Melin.

PINEAPPLE CREAM PIE

½ cup sugar
3 level tablespoons flour
1 level tablespoon corn starch
Pinch salt
2 well beaten egg yolks

1 cup drained crushed pineapple
1 cup boiling water
2 level tablespoons butter
2 egg whites, stiffly beaten

1. Sift sugar, flour, and cornstarch together. 2. Add beaten egg yolks. Stir thoroughly. 3. Add pineapple, boiling water and butter, mix well. 4. Cook in double boiler, stir until very thick. 5. Remove from fire and add egg whites. 6. When cold place in baked pie shell. When ready to serve top with: 1 cup sweet cream whipped mixed with 2 tablespoons sugar and 3 drops lemon extract.

Mary S. Strunk.

ROYAL PUMPKIN PIE

1 baked deep pie shell
1½ cups cooked pumpkin
4 tablespoons flour
1 cup sugar
½ teaspoon salt
1½ teaspoons salt
1½ teaspoons cinnamon

⅔ teaspoon cloves
⅔ teaspoon nutmeg
1 teaspoon ginger
2 eggs
1½ cups milk
¼ cup brown sugar
½ teaspoon vanilla

1. Cook flour, sugar, salt, spices, yolks of eggs and milk in double boiler for 10 minutes, stirring frequently. 2. Add brown sugar to egg whites which have been

beaten and add to cooked mixture. 3. Combine lightly and add vanilla. 4. Pour into bake pie shell and bake in moderate oven. 5. Cool before serving.

Mrs. C. F. Drewes, Dunkirk, N. Y.

RAISIN PIE

¾ cup raisins
¾ cup Grapenuts
¼ cup vinegar
2 tablespoons butter

2¼ cups boiling water
1½ cups brown sugar
Nuts
Salt

1. Cook until thick. 2. Put into pie shell when cool and cover with top crust.
3. Bake in oven 375° F.

Mrs. E. W. Christoffers.

BANBERRY TARTS

1. Roll rich pie crust thin. 2. Cut into rounds with large cookie cutter. On each put a spoonful of filling. 3. Fold over. 4. Pinch edges together. 5. Prick with fork.

Filling

1 cup seeded chopped raisins
1 cup brown sugar
1 egg
Salt
1 tablespoon butter

2 tablespoons cracker crumbs
Grated rind and juice of
1 lemon
Add nuts if desired

1. Boil slowly until thick, stirring constantly.

Clara D. Wheelock.

TOFFEE TARTS

Pie crust
Walnut meats

Seedless raisins
Shredded cocoanut

1. Line patty pans half way up with pie crust. 2. Cut 2 walnuts meats into each pan and add 10 or 12 raisins, add a pinch of shredded cocoanut. 3. Pour over each a tablespoon of the following mixture.

2 eggs
2 cups light brown sugar
1 tablespoon melted butter

½ teaspoon salt
1 teaspoon vanilla

1. Beat together well. This makes about 14 tarts. 2. Bake in a slow oven until crust is done and they are golden brown. Dates may be used in place of raisins.

Olive S. Rykert.

ICEBOX PUDDINGS and CAKES . . .

CARAMEL CHARLOTTE

¾ cup sugar, browned
1 tablespoon gelatine dissolved
   in ¼ cup cold water

1 pint cold milk
Yolks of 5 eggs, beaten
1 pint whipping cream

1. Place cold milk and yolks in double boiler. When hot, add browned sugar and gelatine. 2. Allow the above to get thoroughly cold. 3. Add vanilla and whipped cream. 4. Line pan with lady fingers or sponge cake.

Jennie Green.

GRAHAM CRACKER ROLL

2 cups graham crackers rolled fine
2 cups diced marshmallows
1 cup ground walnuts
1 box dates put through food grinder
½ cup cream
Whipped cream

1. Combine and make into a long roll and cover with more of graham cracker crumbs. 2. Leave in refrigerator over night. 3. Serve with whipped cream.

Mrs. Harry Melin.

GRAPE ICEBOX CAKE

3 tablespoons quick cooking tapioca
2 cups hot grape juice
1 cup sugar
¼ cup orange juice
1 small bottle maraschino cherries
1½ dozen ladyfingers

1. Cook the tapicoa in the grape juice 15 minutes. Stir in the sugar. 2. Remove from heat and add the orange juice, cherry juice, and chopped cherries. Let stand until cool but not thick. 3. Line a ring mould with ladyfingers. Pour part of the above mixture over ladyfingers and continue making alternate layers of ladyfingers and grape mixture until all is used. 4. Place in refrigerator to chill. 5. When ready to serve, remove from mold, fill center, with whipped cream and top with cherries.

Gladys S. Quist.

MARSHMALLOW DESSERT

1 envelope Knox gelatine, dissolved in 1 cup boiling water
1 cup sugar
4 egg whites, beaten to a stiff froth

1. When gelatine is dissolved, add sugar and then egg whites to this mixture and beat 20 minutes or until it looks dry. 2. Divide the mixture, color one-half yellow. 3. Flavor both parts with lemon to taste. 4. Pour yellow part into mold and pour white part over this and place in refrigerator to harden. Serve in slices with custard dessing.

Custard Dressing

1 quart milk
3 egg yolks
3 tablespoons cornstarch
1 cup sugar
Salt

1. Beat egg yolks well. 2. Add a little cold milk, then add sugar, cornstarch and salt. Beat. 3. Add mixture slowly to milk which has been heated in double boiler. 4. Stir constantly until it thickens. Cool. 5. Add 1 teaspoon vanilla. 6. Add yellow coloring if desired. 7. Pour over dessert when ready to serve.

Mrs. Blair, Union City, Pa.

MARSHMALLOW TOAST

6 large cocoanut macaroons
1 tablespoon Knox gelatine
1 cup boiling water
¾ cup sugar
1½ teaspoons orange flavoring
3 egg whites
1 cup crushed pineapple
Nut meats
Whipped cream

1. Soak gelatine in 2 tablespoons pineapple juice for 5 minutes. 2. Dissolve in boiling water. 3. Add sugar. 4. Set in refrigerator until it begins to jelly. 5. Add beaten egg whites and beat until creamy. 6. Add pineapple, nuts and macaroons broken in pieces. 7. Place in ice box for a few hours. 8. Serve with whipped cream.

Mrs. Robert Gardner.

ORANGE CHARLOTTE

1⅓ tablespoons granulated gelatine
⅓ cup cold water
⅓ cup boiling water
1 cup sugar

3 tablespoons lemon juice
1 cup orange juice and pulp
3 egg whites
½ pint heavy cream

1. Soak gelatine in cold water, dissolve in boiling water. 2. Strain and add sugar, lemon juice, orange juice and pulp. 3. Chill in pan of ice water and when quite thick beat until frothy. 4. Add egg whites beaten stiff and fold in whipped cream. 5. Chill thoroughly and serve with soft boiled custard.

Mrs. Bruce Ritenburg.

PINEAPPLE FLUFF

1 package raspberry Jello
1 pint vanilla ice cream

1 small can crushed pineapple

1. Prepare the jello in the usual way. When thick, whip until foamy. 2. Add the ice cream, one tablespoon at a time. 3. Add the pineapple and continue beating. 4. Place in refrigerator to stiffen.

Mrs. L. H. Bittner.

PINEAPPLE ICEBOX PUDDING

¼ pound butter
1 cup confectionery sugar
2 eggs
½ pint whipping cream

1 cup well drained crushed pineapple
½ pound vanilla wafers

1. Cream the butter and sugar together. Add the beaten egg yolks. 2. Fold together the ½ pint cream whipped until stiff, egg whites stiffly beaten, pineapple and creamed mixture. 3. Crumble the wafers and put a layer of crumbs on the bottom of the freezing tray, then add a layer of pineapple mixture and another layer of crumbs, alternating until all ingredients are used, having crumbs for top layer. 4. Freeze.

Dora Douglass.

PINEAPPLE PUDDING

1 small can crushed pineapple
1½ cups water
½ cup sugar
2 eggs

2 tablespoons cornstarch
Pinch of salt
½ pint whipping cream

1. Put water, sugar, eggs, salt, pineapple and cornstarch in double boiler. 2. Cook until real thick. Allow to cool, then add to cream. 3. Place in refrigerator to cool. Do not freeze.

Mildred Rogger.

RIBBON ICEBOX CAKE

1 package cherry Jello
12 graham crackers
½ cup powdered sugar
¼ cup butter, melted

1 egg
½ cup crushed pineapple, drained
¼ cup broken nut meats

1. Prepare the Jello in the usual way and set aside to cool. 2. Crush the graham crackers and place a layer of the crumbs in the bottom of a mold or loaf pan. 3. Combine the sugar, melted butter, beaten egg yolk, pineapple, nuts and the stiffly beaten egg white and alternate this mixture with the crumbs until all ingredients are used. There should be two layers of the filling and three layers of crumbs. 4. When the Jello has started to stiffen, pour half of it over the above and allow it to set. Whip the remaining Jello to a froth and pour over top. Let stand overnight. 5. Slice and serve with whipped cream.

Mrs. Fred Bullock.

PUDDINGS . . .

APPLE CRISP

4 apples
½ cup butter
1 cup brown sugar

1 cup flour
Cinnamon

1. Butter baking dish and cover with apples which have been pared and sliced. 2. Add about ¼ cup water. 3. Blend together sugar, butter and flour, and spread these crumbs over apples. 4. Sprinkle with cinnamon. 5. Bake in moderate oven till apples are done. 6. Serve with plain cream.

Jane Custer.

APPLE GRAHAM DESSERT

2½ cups apple sauce
Brown sugar
Cinnamon

18 graham crackers
¼ cup melted butter

1. Place apple sauce in buttered baking dish. 2. Sprinkle generously with brown sugar and cinnamon. 3. Blend graham cracker crumbs with melted butter and spread on apple sauce. 4. Brown in moderate oven. Serve hot or cold with plain or whipped cream.

Margaret Gailewicz.

BUTTERSCOTCH PUDDING

2 cups brown sugar
2 cups cold water
2 tablespoons cornstarch

1 cup chopped nuts
1 tablespoon butter
1 teaspoon vanilla

1. Dissolve sugar in water and heat to boiling point. 2. Add cornstarch and boil 5 minutes until thick. 3. Remove from fire, add nut meats and butter. 4. Pour in glasses and serve with whipped cream.

Marguerite F. Britz.

CHOCOLATE PUDDING

1 quart milk
½ cup grated chocolate
2 eggs
½ cup sugar
Pinch of salt

2 heaping tablespoons cornstarch
Vanilla
Cream

1. Heat milk in double boiler. When boiling add chocolate. 2. Beat other ingredients together and add to mixture in boiler. Cook until thick. Serve with plain or whipped cream.

Jean Sessions

CHRISTMAS PUDDING

1 cup suet (chopped fine)
1 cup sweet milk
1 cup raisins (chopped)
3 cups flour
  Salt

1 cup sugar
1 can cherries (fruit only)
½ cup walnut meats
1 teaspoon soda

Steam 3 hours.

Whipped Cream Sauce

1 cup brown sugar
  Whites of 2 eggs

1 tablespoon butter
½ pint cream

Cream sugar and butter in double boiler. Add whites of 2 eggs beaten and cook till thick. Let mixture cool and stir in cream whipped.

Jeanette Tuohy.

COTTAGE PUDDING

1 egg
¼ cup butter
2 teaspoons baking powder
⅔ cup milk

1 cup flour
½ cup canned cherries, currants or berries

1. Mix and bake. 2. Serve with sauce flavored with juice of fruit used.

Mrs. William Schuler.

DATE PUDDING

1 cup bread crumbs
1 cup milk
¾ cup sugar
1 cup dates, chopped

1 cup nuts, chopped
2 eggs, beaten
1 teaspoon baking powder
Pinch of salt

1. Beat thoroughly. 2. Bake in flat dish 20 minutes. 3. Serve with cream.

Ruby Stewart.

DELIGHTFUL DESSERT

½ cup sugar
¼ cup butter
4 egg yolks
1 cup sifted flour

4 tablespoons milk
1 teaspoon baking powder
1 pint vanilla ice cream

1. Cream butter and sugar. 2. Add beaten egg yolks and other ingredients. 3. Put this batter in two well greased round cake tins. 4. Pour meringue on top of this and sprinkle with chopped nuts. 5. Bake in moderate oven 20 minutes. Cool. When ready to serve, put layers together with vanilla ice cream. Serves six.

Meringue

4 stiffly beaten egg whites
1 cup sugar

1 teaspoon vanilla
Nut meats

Betty Bowen.

DISH OF SNOW

1 cup cream
¼ pound peanut brittle
1 cup dry boiled rice
1 cup diced pineapple

2 tablespoons pineapple juice
5 marshmallows
1 tablespoon powdered sugar

1. Whip cream and fold in ground brittle. 2. Fold in rice, pineapple and marshmallows. 3. Add sugar. 4. Serve very cold.

Mary Dunbar.

FIG TAPIOCA

½ pound figs, chopped
4 tablespoons minute tapioca

3 cups boiling water
1½ cups brown sugar

1. Cook in double boiler 1 hour, stirring at first to prevent lumping. 2. Cool and serve with whipped cream and nut meats.

Anna G. Hall.

GARIBALDI PUDDING

5 eggs
1 pint cream
1 cup sugar

Juice and rind of 1 lemon
2 tablespoons gelatine
Whipped cream

1. Soak gelatine in ½ cup cold water then set in pan of boiling water and dissolve. 2. Beat egg yolks well and add sugar, juice and rind of lemon. 3. Beat until thick. 4. Add cream which has been whipped. 5. Add gelatine and beaten egg whites. 6. Serve with whipped cream.

Mrs. Harry Melin.

GRAPENUT PUDDING

1 cup grapenuts
2 eggs
Pinch salt

1 quart milk
¼ cup sugar

1. Heat milk and pour over grapenuts. 2. Let stand until the grapenuts soften.
3. Separate the eggs, cream the yolks and sugar. 4. Add to milk mixture.
5. Beat whites and stir into the mixture, add salt. 6. Serve with lemon sauce.

Mrs. William Schuler.

HASTY PUDDING

1 cup brown sugar
½ cup boiling water

1 tablespoon vanilla
1 large lump of butter

1. Place the above ingredients in pudding pan.

Batter

½ cup sugar
¾ cup flour
½ cup milk
1 teaspoon baking powder

Pinch of salt
½ cup nut meats
½ cup raisins

1. Drop batter by spoonfuls over top of sauce in pudding pan. 2. Bake ½ hour, and serve with whipped cream.

Maude Aten, Lincoln, Neb.

LEMON PUDDING

1 cup sugar
2 tablespoons butter
2 egg yolks, beaten
1 cup milk

Rind and juice of one lemon
2 tablespoons flour
2 egg whites, beaten

1. Cream sugar and butter. 2. Add eggs, milk, juice and rind of lemon. 3. Add flour. 4. Fold in beaten egg whites. 5. Bake 30 minutes in medium oven in pan of water. Serves 4.

Norinne Walker.

OLD FASHIONED APPLE PUDDING

Sliced apples
1 cup brown sugar

Nutmeg
½ cup boiling water

1. Grease two quart size baking dish and fill with sliced apples. 2. Sprinkle sugar over top, also nutmeg. 3. Add water, cover and cook over low fire.

Covering

1 cup flour
1 teaspoon baking powder
½ teaspoon salt

¼ cup melted shortening
1 egg
2 tablespoons milk

1. Blend flour sifted with baking powder and salt with shortening and add remaining ingredients. 2. Roll and pat out to cover apples. 3. Bake in oven 350° ½ to ¾ of an hour. — Serve apple side up with brown sugar and whipped cream, sprinkle with nutmeg.

Edna Fuller.

ORANGE CAKE PUDDING

3 eggs
Rind and juice of 1 orange
and ½ lemon

1 cup sugar
1 heaping tablespoon flour
1 cup milk

1. Separate eggs and beat yolks well. 2. Grate rind of orange and ½ lemon and add juice of each. 3. Sift sugar with flour. 4. Add milk. 5. Fold stiffly beaten egg whites into mixture. 6. Butter shallow pan and bake over pan of water 45 minutes in moderate oven. When done place in ice-box and serve with whipped cream.

Rhea Stevens.

PINEAPPLE FLUFF

½ pound marshmallows
1 scant cup of milk
1 pint whipping cream

10c can pineapple, drained well
Graham crackers

1. Melt marshmallows in milk in double boiler. Cool. 2. Add whipped cream and pineapple. 3. Mix and put in dish with layer of graham crackers on top and bottom. — Serves ten.

Maude Aten, Lincoln, Neb.

ROYAL CREAM

1 pint milk
1 tablespoon gelatine dissolved
in ¼ cup cold water

2 eggs
⅓ cup sugar

1. Heat milk and beaten egg yolks to custard consistency. 2. Add sugar and gelatine while hot. 3. Let cool and add beaten egg whites, 1 teaspoon vanilla and pinch of salt. 4. Serve with whipped cream.

Mrs. H. M. Douglass.

SNOW PUDDING

Juice of 1 lemon
6 tablespoons cornstarch
Pinch of salt

1 cup sugar
2 cups water
Whites of 2 eggs

1. Cook in double boiler until clear and thick. 2. Add to the beaten whites or eggs.

Custard Sauce

2 cups milk
Yolks of 2 eggs
Flavoring

⅓ cup sugar
1 teaspoon cornstarch
Pinch of salt

1. Mix and place in double boiler, cook till thick.

Loretta Taft.

TAPICOA PUDDING

6 tablespoons minute tapioca
½ cup sugar
2 eggs
¼ teaspoon salt

1 quart milk
1 tablespoon butter
1 teaspoon vanilla

1. Soak tapicoa in 1 cup milk for ½ hour. 2. Add beaten egg yolks, sugar, salt, butter and remainder of milk. 3. Cook until the mixture thickens, stirring constantly. 4. Add vanilla. 5. Put in pudding dish, cover with meringue of the egg whites, and brown in oven. — Serves six.

Frances H. Kerr.

UNCOOKED PLUM PUDDING

1 package orange Jello
¾ cup sugar
2 cups boiling water
1 cup raisins
1 cup chopped dates

¾ cup currants
1¼ cups nut meats
1 teaspoon cinnamon
¼ teaspoon cloves

1. Pour the boiling water over the sugar and gelatine. Stir and set aside to cool. 2. Cook the raisins in a very little water until soft. Cool. 3. Add the rest of the ingredients with the raisins to the gelatine. 4. Pour into a ring mold and set in the refrigerator to chill but not freeze. 5. Serve with whipped cream.

Lois M. Thompson

STEAMED PUDDINGS . . .

CARROT PUDDING

1 cup grated raw carrots
1 cup grated raw potatoes
1 cup chopped suet
1 cup brown sugar
1 cup raisins
1 cup currants

1 teaspoon soda
1 teaspoon cinnamon
1 teaspoon cloves
1 teaspoon salt
1 teaspoon nutmeg
1½ cups flour

Steam 3 hours.   Serve with hard sauce or cream and sugar.

May Hayward

PLUM DUFF

2 well beaten eggs
½ cup shortening
1 cup brown sugar
1 cup flour

1 large cup mashed prunes
(cook prunes until soft, pit
and mash)
1 teaspoon soda
1 tablespoon milk

Steam 2 hours.   Serve with the following sauce:

1 cup powdered sugar
½ cup butter

¼ cup cream
Flavor with wine or vanilla

This pudding may be steamed a day or two before needed, then re-steamed.

Josephine S. Brand

PLUM PUDDING

1 cup raisins
1 cup currants
¼ pound citron
1 ounce candied orange peel
1 cup flour
1 cup sweet milk
2 cups fine bread crumbs

½ cup suet
½ cup molasses
Mixed spices
1 teaspoon soda (dissolved in
hot water)
3 eggs, whipped light

1. Mix flour and bread crumbs.   2. Dredge fruit with flour mixture.   3. Mix all liquids and add to the flour mixture and beat hard.   4. Pour into well greased pans and steam 4 hours.   5. Both hard and liquid sauce are used. Just before serving, pour brandy over pudding, light and serve.

Mary S. Strunk.

STEAMED CHOCOLATE PUDDING

½ cup sugar
1 egg
½ cup milk
1 cup flour

1 teaspoon baking powder
2 squares melted chocolate
or 2 tablespoons cocoa
1 tablespoon butter

1. Mix together thoroughly.   2. Place in buttered pan.   3. Steam 1 hour. 4. Serve with whipped cream or hard souce.

Mrs. Bruce Ritenburg, Dunkirk, N. Y.

ST. JAMES PUDDING

3 tablespoons butter
1⅔ cups flour
¼ teaspoon salt
¼ teaspoon cloves
¼ teaspoon allspice

¼ teaspoon nutmeg
½ cup corn syrup
½ cup milk
½ teaspoon soda
½ pound dates, cut up

1. Melt the butter, add syrup, milk, sifted dry ingredients and the dates.   2. Turn into a buttered mold and steam 2½ or 3 hours. Serve with the following sauce.

Orange Foamy Sauce:

½ cup butter
2 eggs

1 cup sugar
1 orange, grated rind and juice

Cream the butter and sugar and add the egg yolks. Cook in double boiler until it thickens and pour over the beaten whites of eggs.

Mrs. Elmer E. Smith.

STEAMED PUDDING I

1 cup brown sugar
½ cup shortening
1 egg
Salt
1 teaspoon cinnamon

1 teaspoon cloves
Rounding cup of flour
1 teaspoon soda
½ cup sour milk
1 cup chopped raisins

Steam 2 hours.

Sauce

1 egg
Confectionery sugar

Vanilla
½ pint whipping cream

1. Mix egg with confectionery sugar until rather stiff. 2. Add vanilla and last cream whipped. 3. Serve on pudding.

Ida Weaver.

STEAMED PUDDING II

1 cup brown sugar
½ cup shortening
1 egg
½ cup sour milk
1 teaspoon soda
1 cup raisins or dates

½ cup nuts
½ teaspoon cinnamon
½ teaspoon vanilla
½ teaspoon salt
1½ cups flour

1. Cream sugar and shortening together. 2. Add egg. 3. Dissolve soda in milk then add to the mixture. 4. Add raisins (chopped) nuts, cinnamon, vanilla, salt, and flour. 5. Steam 3 hours. 6. Serve with sauce.

Sauce

1 tablespoon soft butter
1 cup powdered sugar

1 egg yolk
½ pint cream

1. Beat mixture white. 2. Add to cream whipped.

Mrs. Kenneth Lovelee, Dunkirk, N. Y.

STEAMED SUET PUDDING

1 cup molasses
1 cup suet
1 cup raisins
1 large apple
1 cup sour milk

1 teaspoon soda
1 teaspoon salt
1 teaspoon cinnamon
3 cups flour

1. Chop suet, raisins and apple. 2. Stir soda in sour milk. 3. Blend all ingredients. 4. Steam 3 hours.

Mrs. H. S. Rykert.

SAUCES FOR PUDDINGS and ICE CREAM . . .

BUTTERSCOTCH SAUCE I

1 cup granulated sugar
1 cup Blue Label corn syrup

1 cup cream

1. Cook in double boiler 1 hour. 2. Add pinch of salt and 2 tablespoons butter.
Mrs. C. F. Drewes, Dunkirk, N. Y.

BUTTERSCOTCH SAUCE II

1 cup sugar
1 cup maple syrup
1 tablespoon flour

½ cup cream
2 tablespoons butter

Mix flour and sugar. Add the maple sugar and boil for a few minutes. Add ½ cup cream and 2 tablespoons butter.

Marie Johnston.

GREEN MINT SAUCE

1 cup strained honey
2 egg whites

½ teaspoon peppermint extract
Green coloring

1. Cook honey 7 minutes. After it begins to boil pour slowly on stiffly beaten egg whites, continue beating until stiff. 2. Flavor with the peppermint and tint a delicate green. Use this sauce for chocolate ice cream.

Clara B. Sessions.

HOT CHOCOLATE SAUCE

2 cups cocoa
7 cups sugar
1 pound bitter chocolate

1 quart coffee cream
1½ pounds butter

1. Melt chocolate in double boiler, add butter, sugar and cocoa and stir until melted. 2. Add a little cream at a time stirring constantly. 3. Cook 2 minutes then add more cream. 4. Makes 1 gallon. Especially good with ice cream.

Maude Aten, Lincoln, Nebraska.

OTHER DESSERTS . . .

ANGEL PIE

4 egg whites
Pinch of salt
½ teaspoon cream of tartar

1 cup sugar
Fresh fruit
½ pint whipping cream

1. Beat the egg whites to a froth, add salt and cream of tartar and beat some more. 2. Add sugar, 1 tablespoon at a time, beating all the while. 3. Grease a pie tin and dust with flour. 4. Pour in mixture and bake in slow oven 250°) for 1 hour on the top grate. 5. To serve, fill with fresh fruit and top with whipped cream, or fill with ice cream and top with fresh fruit.

Dora Douglass.

APPLE CAKE

1½ cups flour
2 teaspoons baking powder
½ teaspoon salt
2 tablespoons shortening

½ cup milk
4 or 5 apples
½ cup sugar
1 teaspoon cinnamon

1. Sift together dry ingredients. 2. Rub in shortening lightly. 3. Add milk and mix. 4 Place dough on board and pat out ½ inch thick. 5. Place in pie tin and press apples into dough. 6. Sprinkle with sugar and cinnamon. 7. Bake in moderate oven 30 minutes or until apples are done.

Mrs. J. C. Boody.

APRICOT FILLED ANGEL CAKE

1 whole angel food cake
2 cups apricot puree made from cooked, unsweetened
dried apricots
1 cup water
1 package lemon Jello

1. Add puree to water, boil, add Jello and stir until dissolved. 2. Cut the center out of the cake leaving a border thick enough to give a generous slice. 3. When apricot mixture is partially firm, pour into the center of the cake. 4. Chill thoroughly. 5. When ready to serve, ice the sides and top with whipped cream.

Lois M. Thompson

BLITZ TORTE

½ cup butter
½ cup sugar
4 tablespoons milk
Yolks of 4 eggs
1 teaspoon vanilla
1 cup flour
1 teaspoon baking powder

1. Mix and spread in 2 layers. 2. On top of each layer before baking spread the following after combining:

1 cup sugar
½ teaspoon vanilla
4 egg whites beaten stiff
½ teaspoon almond

1. Bake in steady oven ½ hour. (350° to 375°).

Filling

½ cup milk
1 teaspoon cornstarch
1 teaspoon vanilla
1 egg
2 teaspoons sugar
1 teaspoon butter

1. Put frosting side down, on bottom of cake and upon top, with filling between.

Marguerite Taft.

NUT JELLY

6 tablespoons minute tapioca
½ teaspoon salt
Nuts
Dates
3 cups hot water
2 cups brown sugar
Vanilla

1. Put hot water and salt in double boiler, stir in tapioca and sugar. 2. Cook until clear, about 45 minutes; stir frequently. 3. Turn into bowl and when cool add nuts, dates and vanilla. 4. Serve with whipped cream.

Mrs. Walter Taylor.

ORANGE DELIGHT

1½ cups orange juice
1 cup whipping cream
25 marshmallows

1. Heat orange juice to boiling. 2. Add marshmallows and stir until they are dissolved. 3. Cool. 4. Stir in the stiffly beaten cream and chill.

Mrs. Robert D. Sprague.

RUSK TART

1 package Holland Rusk	1½ cups sugar
½ teaspoon cinnamon	½ cup melted butter

1. Roll rusk fine, reserve ½ cup for top.   2. Mix remaining with above.   3. Line pie tin with mixture.

2 cups stewed apples	1 lemon
2 eggs	1 cup sugar
1 teaspoon corn starcn	½ pint cream

1. Place apples, eggs, juice of lemon, and sugar over fire and bring to a boil. 2. Add corn starch mixed with a little water, boil 1 minute..   3. Pour in tin. 4. Whip ½ pint cream and put on top, and the remaining ½ cup Holland Rusk over all.   This will keep several days.

Mrs. Charles Grover.

STRAWBERRY FLUFF

1 egg white	1 cup confectioners sugar
1 cup hulled and cut straw-	
berries	

1. Beat 20 minutes.   2. Serve on angel food cake or in compotes.

Mrs. E. W. Christoffers.

UPSIDE DOWN GINGERBREAD

½ cup raisins	½ cup brown sugar
1 cup crushed pineapple	2 tablespoons butter

1. Let four ingredients simmer while mixing the gingerbread.

½ cup sugar	1 teaspoon cinnamon
½ cup butter or shortening	1 teaspoon ginger
1 egg	Pinch of cloves
1 cup molasses	2½ cups flour, measured after
1½ teaspoons soda	sifting
½ teaspon salt	1 cup hot water

1. Pour first mixture into well-buttered iron skillet.   2. Cover with gingerbread mixture.   3. Bake.   4. Turn upside down while hot.   5. Serve with whipped cream.

Mrs. Blair, Union City, Pa.

CANDIES . . .

FONDANT

2 cups sugar
1¼ cups water

2 tablespoons corn syrup

1. Boil all ingredients until soft ball is formed when dropped in cold water. 2. Take from fire and pour in cold pan. 3. When real cold, stir until soft and creamy. 4. Cover with wet cloth until used.

Ethel Conaway.

OPERA CREAMS

3 cups sugar
1 cup cream
1 teaspoon vanilla

⅓ teaspoon cream of tartar
1 cup nuts

1. Mix cream, sugar and cream of tartar. 2. Cook without stirring until very soft ball is formed when tested in cold water. 3. Pour at once on large platter which has been moistened with water. Do not move dish after candy is in it. 4. When syrup is cool add vanilla (coloring if desired). 5. Beat with wooden spoon until creamy and stiff. 6. Knead with hands until soft. 7. Add nuts. 8. Shape.

Katherine Regan Kane.

PEANUT BRITTLE

Shelled peanuts
2 cups sugar
Pinch soda

Lump of butter
1 teaspoon vanilla

1. Cover bottom of greased pan with peanuts. 2. Put sugar in iron frying pan. 3. Dissolve over hot fire stirring constantly 4. When dissolved add soda, butter and vanilla. 5. Pour over peanuts.

Ethel Conaway.

PEANUT CLUSTERS

Dot Chocolate

Peanuts

1. Melt chocolate in double boiler. 2. Stir in shelled peanuts. 3. Drop by spoonfuls on waxed paper. — You may use cocoanut instead of nuts.

Ethel Conaway.

SOUR CREAM FUDGE

2 cups sugar
1 ten-cent can Hershey's syrup
1 cup sour cream

1 teaspoon vanilla
Salt

1. Mix sugar, salt and syrup. 2. When hot add sour cream gradually. 3. Boil without stirring, to soft ball stage. 4. Cool, add vanilla and beat until thick.

Mrs. Jackson B. Clark

JELLIES and PRESERVES . . .

CRANBERRY CONSERVE

1 quart cranberries
½ cup water
4 cups sugar

1 orange, ground fine
½ cup raisins
½ cup walnuts

1. Put the cranberries and the water on a slow fire and let "pop". 2. Add 2 cups sugar and let dissolve. 3. Add 2 more cups and 1 orange cut or ground fine, the raisins and walnuts. 4. Boil a few minutes and put in glasses.

Mabel Edmunds.

CRANBERRY MARMALADE

1 pound cranberries
2 oranges

2 cups sugar

1. Put cranberries through food chopper. 2. Add orange juice and rind of one. 3. Two cups of sugar add and mix well. 4. Let stand for 24 hours. 5. Seal for future use if desired.

Mary E. Cook.

FIG JAM

4 pounds pears
3 pounds sugar

1 pound figs
½ pound walnuts

1. Grind but do not peel pears. 2. Add sugar, cook in slow oven 2 hours. 3. Stir often, add 1 pound ground figs; cook another hour. 4. Add nuts chopped. Excellent filling for cakes or cookies.

Mrs. Fred Barrett

GINGER PEAR

4 pounds pears
4 pounds sugar
1 small cup water

2 lemons (juice)
3 ounces crystalized ginger

1. Wash, peel quarter, slice pears. 2. Add sugar and water. 3. Boil pears until tender. 4. Add juice of lemons, and ginger. 5. Boil until thick.

Jessie Hillman.

GINGER PEAR CHIPS

8 pounds pears (sliced thin)
6 pounds sugar
1½ pints water

Grated rind and juice of
2 lemons
25 cent jar preserved ginger root

1. Slice pears, rind and juice of lemon, water and sugar. Boil all together 1½ hours. 2. Add ginger root cut up. 3. Boil ½ hour longer and can.

Mrs. R. H. Watson

GRAPE CONSERVE I

3 pounds grapes
1 pound raisins

1 pound walnut meats
3 pounds sugar

1. Separate pulp from skins. 2. Heat pulp enough to loosen seeds, put through sieve. 3. Add sugar, skins, raisins and nuts. 4. Cook until thick.

Mrs. H. M. Douglass

GRAPE CONSERVE II

½ peck grapes
2 oranges (juice and rind)
2 lemons (juice and rind)

1 cup chopped nuts
Sugar
½ teaspoon salt

1. Wash grapes before removing skins. 2. Remove skins from pulp. Soak pulp until soft. Strain to remove seeds. 3. Put strained pulp in kettle. 4. Extract juice from oranges and lemons. Put rind through the food chopper. Add to grape mixture. 5 .Cook for 1 hour. 6. Measure and take equal quantity of sugar. 7. Add nuts and salt; pour into glasses and seal while hot.

Marion Mackie.

GRAPE JELLY

1 twenty-pound basket
Concord grapes

5 pounds granulated sugar

1. Stem grapes, wash berries. 2. Place in preserving kettle adding enough water to prevent scorching. 3. Stew until berries have burst. Drain in cloth sieve, squeeeze slightly. 4. Place juice over fire. Boil. 5. Add sugar and cook until contents will jelly from spoon. Makes at least 25 small glasses. It is best to make two boilings of juice. More sugar may be added if grapes are sour.

Lotta L. Deane

ORANGE, GRAPEFRUIT AND LEMON MARMALADE

1 orange
1 grapefruit
1 lemon

Water
Sugar

1. Cut fruit in small pieces. 2. Add 3 times as much water as fruit and boil 10 minutes. Let stand over night. 3. Next morning boil until tender 4. Add equal amounts of sugar and cook until thick.

Mrs. Daniel Harmon

PEACH CONSERVE

18 peaches
1 can crushed pineapple

1 bottle Maraschino cherries
2 cups sugar

1. Wash and cut up fruit. 2. Add sugar. 3 Mix well. 4. Boil slowly about 45 minutes until thick.

Olive S. Rykert

PEACH AND ORANGE MARMALADE

2½ pounds peaches
2½ pounds sugar

3 oranges
1 lemon

1. Wash and peel peaches, cut into small pieces. 2. Add sugar and boil until half done. 3. Put in juice of 3 oranges, grated rind of one orange, shaved peel of 2 oranges. Juice of lemon and rind. 4. Boil until thick.

Jessie Hillman

PEACH JAM I

12 peaches
3 oranges
Sugar

1 bottle Maraschino cherries
(sliced)

1. Cut up peaches and oranges.   2. Measure fruit with cup, and add same amount of sugar as there is fruit.   3. Cook fruit and sugar slowly until it begins to thicken and then add cherries.   4. Put in glasses.   This recipe makes 6 or 7 glasses.

Ethel S. Graf

PEACH JAM II

1 quart diced peaches
1 No. 2 can crushed pineapple
5 cups sugar
Juice and ½ grated rind of

2 oranges
Juice of 1 lemon
1 cup nuts
1 large bottle maraschino
cherries

1. Cut and dice peaches.   2. Add sugar and juice and rind of oranges and juice of lemon, pineapple.   3. Boil until thick stirring frequently to keep from scorching.   4. Remove from the fire, add nuts and cherries, boil slightly before pouring into glasses.

Eva Clark

PEACH AND PINEAPPLE JAM

2 pounds fruit, equal parts
both
3 pounds sugar

1 lemon (juice and rind)
1 orange (juice and rind)
½ bottle Certo

1. Peel peaches.   2. Add same amount crushed pineapple.   3. Put in sugar, juice and rind of one orange, and one lemon.   4. Boil and add ½ small bottle Certo.   5. Put in glasses when thick.

Mrs. Russel Lawrence, Dunkirk, N. Y.

PINEAPPLE AND STRAWBERRY PRESERVES

3 cups sugar
1 cup fresh pineapple cut in

2 cups whole strawberries
small pieces

Boil rapidly 6 - 8 minutes.

Marie Johnston

STRAWBERRY JAM I

2 quarts strawberries
4 cups sugar

2 cups sugar

1. Wash and hull berries.   2. Scald berries and let boiling water stand on them 2 minutes.   3. Drain thoroughly.   4. Add 4 cups sugar, boil 2 minutes after full boil is reached.   5. Set off stove and when bubbling stops add 2 more cups sugar.   6. Boil 5 minutes after full boil is reached.   7. Pour into shallow pan and let stand over night.   Put in jars and seal.

Mrs. Ferdinand Sievert

STRAWBERRY JAM II

2 cups crushed strawberries   3 cups granulated sugar

1. Wash, stem and crush berries.   2. Add sugar and mix well.   3. When mixture comes to rolling boiling point stir constantly for six minutes.   4. Do not try to cook more than this amount at once.   5. As you cook more when taken from the

fire add to the first amount and let it all stand in kettle until cool.   6. Pour into jars and cover with paraffine.

Mrs. E. M. Bowen.

STRAWBERRY PRESERVES

1 quart berries
2 cups sugar

2 cups sugar
2 teaspoons lemon juice

1. Wash berries.   2. Add 2 cups sugar and cook 5 minutes.   3. Add 2 more cups sugar and lemon juice.   4. Cook 10 or 12 minutes.   5 Let stand over night and put in glasses

Mrs. J. S. Stevenson

TOMATO MARMALADE

4 lemons
3 ounces candied ginger
4 quarts tomatoes (measure)
     after skinned

1 tablespoon salt
4 pounds sugar

1. Wash lemons and cut in thin slices.   2. Add ginger cut fine and boil until tender.   3. Add tomatoes.   4. Boil together until mixture is quite thick stirring constantly.   5. Add sugar and boil at least one hour.   6. Keep stirring, test on ice to see if thick enough.   7. Put in jars.

Mrs. Walter Taylor.

WHITE CHERRY PRESERVES

5 quarts white cherries
5 quarts sugar

3 oranges
1 bottle Certo

1. Wash, pit and drain cherries.   2. Add small amount of water, bring to boiling point and drain.   3. Heat the sugar as for jelly and add oranges cut in small pieces without rind.   4. Add cherries, the juice should dissolve the sugar. 5. Boil 15 minutes.   6. Take from stove add 1 bottle Certo.

Mrs. Walter Clark, Brocton, N. Y.

WHITE PLUM CONSERVE

3 dozen plums
3 oranges

Sugar

1. Cut plums into small pieces. Squeeze the juice of the oranges into the plums. 2. Chop the rind and plup very fine.   3. Mix all and add the same amount of sugar.   4. Cook until it thickens and put in jelly glasses.

Emily G. Hayward.

PICKLES and RELISHES . . .

BAKED PICKLED PEACHES

7 pounds peaches
5 pounds granulated sugar

1 pint vinegar
1 ounce cinnamon sticks

1. Wipe peaches with a towel. 2. Pack in stone jar. 3. Make a syrup of vinegar, sugar and cinnamon. 4. Pour over peaches, cover. 5. Bake in moderate oven 350° for 1 hour. — Do not remove cover until you want to use.

Mrs. J. S. Stevenson.

CHUNK PICKLES

7 pounds medium sized
cucumbers
2 tablespoons pulverized alum
3 pounds brown sugar
1 ounce celery seed

1 ounce cassia buds or
cinnamon
½ ounce whole allspice
3 pints vinegar (not too
strong)

1. Soak the cucumbers 3 days in brine strong enough to float an egg. Take out, soak in fresh water 3 days changing the water each day. Wipe dry and cut in chunks. 2. Scald good in weak vinegar, grape leaves and 2 tablespoons of pulverized alum. Omit the grape leaves if you care to. 3. Make a syrup of the vinegar, sugar and spices. Pour over the chunk pickles while hot. Let stand over night and reheat. This will keep in open jar.

Corinne L. Lounsberry.

CUCUMBER PICKLES

300 small pickles
1 gallon vinegar
1 cup sugar
1 cup salt

½ cup grated horseradish
1 teaspoon mustard
1 teaspoon red pepper
1 tablespoon alum

1. Wash and pour boiling water over the cucumbers. Let stand until cold. 2. When cold wipe dry, pack in jars and pour the cold vinegar, spices and alum over them.

Emily G. Hayward.

DELICIOUS PICKLES

Soak cucumbers for nine days or as long as you wish, in brin strong enough to bear an egg. Take from brine soak in cold water for 2 days, changing the water night and morning. Put in kettle and cover with half water and half vinegar, allowing one tablespoonful of powdered alum to each gallon of liquid. Cover closely and simmer about ¾ hour but do not let come to a boil. Remove from kettle and drop in cold water. When entirely cold slice and put in jars draining well.

Make a syrup of the following:

1 quart vinegar
3 pounds brown sugar

2 ounces mixed pickle spices

Pour into jars and seal.

Mrs. John W. Ballard.

DILL PICKLES

100 pickles
3 quarts vinegar
1 quart water

1 large cup salt
¼ teaspoon powdered alum

1. Wash and scrub pickles.　2. Soak in clear cold water over night.　3. Wipe dry.
4. Boil vinegar, water and salt. 5. Put in jar alternating a layer of pickles, a layer
of onion and layer of dill until jar is full.　6. Pour over hot vinegar　solution
with alum. — Seal hot.

Mrs. A. P. Chessman.

END OF GARDEN PICKLES

2 quarts small onions
1 quart of fresh corn
6 or 8 carrots
2 quarts string beans
8 green peppers
4 red peppers

2 ounces celery seed
2 ounces mustard seed
2 dozen small sweet pickles
3 cups sugar
Salt to taste

1. Wash vegetables.　2. Cut carrots lengthwise.　3. Cut pickles lengthwise.
4. Cook all vegetables separately.　5. Mix all together and cover with　vinegar,
add sugar and salt.　6. Let come to a boil and seal.

Mrs. A. P. Chessman.

FRENCH PICKLES

400-500 very small pickles
1 gallon of vinegar (dilute
　if strong)
1 cup sugar
1 cup salt
1 cup grated horseradish or
　1 bottle horseradish

½ cup ground mustard, stirred
　into a paste with water
A handful of mixed spices
or put a few on top of each
can
5 cents worth of saccharine

1. Scrub each pickle well, put in earthen or granite dish, cover with boiling water
and let stand over night.　2. In the morning drain and wipe each pickle dry with
a clean cloth, pack them in jars and pour over them the syrup made from the
above ingredients.

Mrs. J. B. Schoeffel.

GERMAN DILL PICKLES

3 quarts and 1 cupful water
1 cupful vinegar

1 cupful salt
Stalk of dill
Alum

1. Mix above, bring to boil and cool overnight.　2. Fill quart jars with fresh
cucumbers about 3 inches long.　3. Add stalk of dill and two grape
leaves, pinch alum size of apple seed.　4. Pour over pickling liquid and seal jar.

LeOra Weiss.

MUSTARD PICKLE

1 quart small cucumbers
1 quart large cucumbers sliced
2 quarts small onions
1 quart green tomatoes
1 quart large green tomatoes,
　sliced
2 cauliflowers

5 green peppers cut in strips
　(Take out seeds)
½ pound mustard
1 ounce tumeric
6 cups sugar
2 cups flour

1. Wash and slice large cucumbers, tomatoes and cauliflower.　2. Make a paste
of spices, sugar and flour and stir into 1 gallon vinegar (boiling).　3. Soak vege-

tables in salt water, drain and steam them a very little before putting them in the prepared paste.

Jessie Hillman.

PICKLED WHITE ONIONS

Pour strong brine over onions. Let stand 24 hours or longer. Drain and cook in ⅓ vinegar and ⅔ water until tender, not more than 15 minutes. Drain and make a syrup of vinegar, sugar and spices to taste. Take off stove, do not cook. Can hot.

Mrs. C. J. Ellis.

SPICED PEARS

9 pounds pears
1 pint vinegar

1 cup cinnamon and cloves
mixed

1. Peel pears and cut in halves. 2. Let spices and vinegar come to boil. 3. Put in pears, let come to boil. Simmer for 3 hours. 4. Repeat this for 3 days. 5. Put in jars. — Dutchess pears are best — not too ripe.

Alice Monroe, Dunkirk, N. Y.

RELISHES ...

CHILI SAUCE I

30 large ripe tomatoes
12 large apples
6 medium sized onions
2 red peppers (hot)
2 green peppers

3 tablespoons salt
1 teaspoon cinnamon
1 teaspoon cloves
1 quart vinegar
Sugar to taste

1. Peel tomatoes and apples. 2. Chop all together with the peppers and onions. 3. Add vinegar, salt and sugar. 4. Cook over slow fire about 2½ hours. Keep stirring to keep from scorching.

Mrs. Kate Witkowski, Dunkirk, N. Y.

CHILI SAUCE II

12 ripe tomatoes
2 onions
1 green pepper
1 red sweet pepper
¾ cup brown sugar

½ cup vinegar
1 teaspoon cloves
1 teaspoon cinnamon
1 tablespoon salt

1. Wash, peel and slice tomatoes thin. 2. Chop onions and peppers. 3. Add vinegar and sugar. 4. Boil until thick, being careful not to scorch. 5. Add spices just before it is done to keep color.

Olive E. Rykert.

CRANBERRY SAUCE

4 cups cranberries
2 cups boiling water

2 cups sugar

1. Wash cranberries, add boiling water, cook three minutes. 2. Add 2 cups sugar cook 2 minutes. 3. Test by putting drop on cardboard. Let stand one minute.

Tip, if liquid runs cook more. 4. The drop must remain in solid form. 5. Rinse mould or moulds in cold water before pouring in the sauce.

Ida Weaver.

CRANBERRY RELISH

4 cups cranberries
2 oranges

1 lemon
2 cups sugar

1. Wash and pick over cranberries. 2. Wash oranges and lemon. 3. Cut in pieces and put through food chopper, skins and all, together with cranberries. 4. Add sugar and mix well. 5. Chill and let stand 24 hours before serving.

Frances H. Kerr.

EAST INDIA CHUTNEY

12　pounds peaches
2　pounds raisins
½ pound salt
3½ pounds brown sugar
1　green ginger root

¼ pound garlic
½ pound mustard seed
6　small red peppers
3　quarts vinegar

1.Slice peaches into vinegar. 2. Scrape ginger root into very thin slices. 3. Put garlic, red peppers and raisins through meat chopper. 4. Cook peaches until tender. Add other ingredients, cook until tender. (Hot and spicy but very nice).

Mary S. Strunk.

GREEN TOMATO RELISH

2 quarts green tomatoes
3 onions
2 large sweet peppers
1 tablespoon tumeric

2 tablespoons white mustard seed
1 tablespoon salt
3 cups sugar
1 quart weak vinegar

1. Cut tomatoes in pieces. 2. Add onions and pepper after putting through the food chopper. 3. Put in spices, sugar and vinegar with salt. 4. Cook 1 hour, seal hot.

Mrs. E. W. Christoffers.

MOCK MINCE MEAT

3 large apples
3 cups brown sugar
1 cup raisins
1 teaspoon cinnamon

½ cup vinegar
1 teaspoon allspice
1 teaspoon nutmeg
Pinch salt

1. Chop the tomatoes and apples fine. 2. Grind raisins. 3. Mix all together and boil.

Mrs. E. Schwartz, Dunkirk, N. Y.

MOTHER'S GREEN TOMATO MINCE MEAT

1 peck green tomatoes
5 pounds white and brown
　sugar mixed
2 pounds seeded raisins
2 tablespoons cloves
2 tablespoons cinnamon

2 tablespoons allspice
2 tablespoons salt
1 cup vinegar
1 cup chopped suet
3 bowls chopped sour apples

1. Chop green tomatoes coarsely. 2. Drain and add as much water as there was juice 3. Add sugar and raisins. 4. Cook slowly until tomatoes are tender. 5. Add spices, vinegar, salt and suet. 6. Boil until thick, stirring frequently. 7. Add apples and cook until tender. 8. Seal in jars. This recipe makes about 10 pints.

Ethel S. Graf.

PEAR MINCEMEAT

10 pounds chopped pears
4 pounds brown sugar
2 pounds raisins (seedless)
2 pounds currants
1½ cups vinegar

2 tablespoons salt
2 tablespoons cinnamon
2 tablespoons cloves
2 tablespoons nutmeg
2 oranges ground

1. Peel and chop up pears. 2. Add raisins, currants sugar, vinegar and spices with 2 ground oranges. 3. Cook all together until thick. 4. Put into jars and seal. When making pies add 2 tablespoons butter to each.

Eva Clark.

PEPPER HASH

12 green peppers
12 red peppers
12 large onions

1½ pints vinegar
1½ cups sugar
1½ tablespoons salt

1. Grind peppers and onions separately. 2. Pour boiling water over each and let stand 10 minutes. 3. Drain thoroughly. 4. Mix above with vinegar, sugar and salt. 5. Boil 15 minutes put in jars and seal.

Flora Weiler, Dunkirk, N. Y.

UNCOOKED CHILI SAUCE

1 peck ripe tomatoes
6 onions
5 peppers (sweet)
1 pepper (hot)
3 bunches celery

1 cup salt
3 pounds sugar
3 cups vinegar
2 ounces white mustard seed

1. Soak tomatoes, onions, peppers, celery in salt over night. 2. Drain in cloth sack for several hours. 3. Add sugar, vinegar and mustard seed. 4. Can in sterilized jars, seal. Very good in Russian dressing.

Mrs. Fred Bullock.

CANNED CORN

6 cups corn
1 cup salt

⅔ cup sugar

1. Cut corn from cob. 2. Add salt and sugar. 3. Cook 20 minutes in open kettle and seal hot. 4. When ready to serve, parboil ten minutes in clear water. Drain, season with butter and pepper.

Mrs. E. W. Christoffers.

GRAPE JUICE

Wash and stem grapes. Cover with water. Cook slowly until thorougly cooked. Strain through a jelly bag. To one gallon grape juice add three cups sugar (less if grapes are sweet). Return to fire and when boiling, seal in fruit jars or cap in bottles.

Mrs. E. M. Bowen.

TOMATO COCKTAIL

1 quart tomatoes	¼ cup celery leaves and stalk
1 green pepper	1½ teaspoons salt
1 small onion	1 teaspoon horseradish

1. To each quart of tomatoes add pepper chopped or cut, chopped onion, celery, salt and horseradish. 2. Cook together until done. 3. Strain, bring to boiling point and can. Process sealed jars for 5 minutes.

Mrs. Charles Driscoll, Dunkirk, N. Y.

SANDWICHES . . .

CHEESE AND OLIVE

10 cent jar stuffed olives
2 cakes cream cheese
4 hard boiled eggs
2 small onions

Grind ingredients together.

Edna Foss.

CHILDREN'S DELIGHT

4 hard boiled eggs
1 raw carrot, grated
2 pickles
Drop of onion juice

Mix all ingredients together and add mayonnaise to make the right consistency for spreading for sandwiches.

Esther Rabin.

CUCUMBER FILLING

1 cucumber, peeled and seeded
1 package cream cheese
¼ small onion grated
Salt and pepper

Mix all ingredients and color with green coloring. Use on open sandwiches.

Virginia Harmon.

EGG AND CHEESE

3 eggs cooked hard
2 packages cream cheese
2 dill pickles
1 small jar pimentos
2 tablespoons grated onion
Pinch of salt

Chop all ingredients fine and mix with salad dressing.

Mrs. F. E. Himebaugh, Dunkirk.

FRENCH TOAST

Make 2 slices of French toast. Put a slice of baked ham on the toast and cover with Welch Rarebit. Cover with the other slice of toast and serve hot.

Lois M. Thompson.

LIVERWURST FILLING

Liverwurst sausage
Chopped Pickle

Mix together and spread on brown bread.

Dora Douglass

MUSHROOM FILLING

Saute ½ pound of mushrooms in butter and chop fine. Mix 2 cakes cream cheese with mushrooms. If necessary use cream to get mixture the right consistency to spread.

Ida Weaver.

SANDWICH LOAF

Large loaf of bread
Ham filling
Egg and onion filling
Tomato, lettuce and mayonnaise filling
3 cakes cream cheese
Mayonnaise

1. Cut crust from bread. 2. Slice bread long way in four strips. 3. Butter each

strip.   4. Put together with the three fillings in layers.   5. Mix cream cheese and mayonnaise and cover outside as for icing on a cake.   6. Garnish with sliced stuffed olives or yolks of hard-boiled eggs. — Serves 8.

Ethel S. Graf.

SCRAMBLED EGG AND CHEESE

Toast 2 slices of bread and butter them.   Scramble 2 eggs in double boiler. Place on toast and cover with melted cheese.   Serve hot.

Dora Cease.

CHILDREN'S RECIPES . . .

PETER RABBIT SALAD

Lettuce

Canned pears

Shelled peanuts

Cream cheese

1. Arrange lettuce on plates and place one half pear on each bed of lettuce with rounded side up. 2. Soften cream cheese. 3. Wash hands very clean and mold cheese into a little round bunny tail and place at large end of pear, and into a larger head and place at small end of pear. 4. Put a half peanut on each side of head for ears, and if Mother has pink cake coloring, paint pink eyes and nose. This looks like a bunny eating lettuce, and is fun to make.

Billy B. Kerr.

CHOCOLATE FUDGE

2 cups sugar

1 cup milk

2 squares chocolate

Salt

1 tablespoon butter

Vanilla

1 cup nut meats

1. Boil together, sugar milk chocolate and one half the butter until it forms a soft ball in cold water. 2. Remove from fire and let stand 5 minutes. 3. Beat until almost hard enough to pour out, then add the vanilla and nuts, pour into greased pan and cut in squares.

Virginia Harmon.

CRY BABY COOKIES

1 cup sugar

2 tablespoons shortening

2 eggs

1 cup molasses

1 cup sour milk

1 cup raisins

4 cups flour

2 teaspoon soda

1 teaspoon salt

½ teaspoon cloves

½ teaspoon allspice

½ teaspoon ginger

1. Cream shortening and sugar. 2. Add other ingredients, as given. 3. Last add floured raisins. 4. Drop from spoon on greased pan and bake in slow oven.

Jeanne Rabin.

CHOCOLATE CAKE

1 cup sugar

1 egg, beaten

1 cup sour milk

1 teaspoon soda

1½ cups flour

2 squares chocolate melted with 2 tablespoons butter

1 teaspoon vanilla

1. Combine ingredients in order given. 2. Bake slowly in moderate oven.

Ice with Custard

2 squares chocolate

1 tablespoon butter

2 tablespoons cornstarch

1 cup sugar

1½ cups boiling water

Vanilla

1. Cook in double boiler, until thick. 2. Cool and spread on cake.

Jeanne Rabin.

MAMMY'S CORN BREAD

¼ cup sugar	1 cup flour
2 tablespoons butter	¾ cup corn meal
1 egg	4 teaspoons baking powder
1 cup milk	

1. Cream the sugar and butter in a bowl. 2. Beat egg, then add egg and milk. 3. Sift flour, corn meal and baking powder, and add. 4. Beat well. 5. Bake in shallow, greased pan in moderate oven, 350º, for 45 minutes.

Mary B. Sessions.

CHOCOLATE NUT DROPS

1 cup sugar	1½ cups flour
¼ cup butter	2 teaspoons baking powder
1 egg	½ cup cocoa
½ cup milk	1 cup nut meats

1. Cream the sugar and butter in a bowl. 2. Add the beaten egg and milk. 3. Sift flour, baking powder and cocoa and add. 4. Drop by spoonfuls. 5. Bake for 15 minutes at 355º.

Mary Margaret Hoepner
Dunkirk.

FUDGE SAUCE

1½ cups sugar	1 cup water
1 cup cocoa	1 teaspoon vanilla

1. Mix the sugar, cocoa and water in a pan and boil 15 minutes. 2. Cool, then add vanilla. — Delicious over ice cream, cake or pudding.

Sally Hoepner.

HOT CHOCOLATE

1 cup milk	1 tablespoon fudge sauce

1. Heat milk and stir in fudge sauce. 2. Serve with marshmallows.

Nancy Ann Hoepner.

CHOCOLATE FUDGE

2 cups sugar	2 tablespoons butter
½ cocoa	1 teaspoon vanilla
1 cup milk	

1. Put cocoa, milk and butter in saucepan. 2. Mix well. 3. Cook for 15 minutes slowly. 4. Remove from fire and beat hard until creamy. 5. Add vanilla. 6. Pour into shallow buttered pan to cool.

Barbara Stevens.

HOUSEHOLD HINTS...

Vegetables grown underground should be cooked in fresh water. Those grown above ground in salted water.

In preparing apples for salad, etc., drop them in salt water to prevent tarnishing. One teaspoon salt to a quart.

A small amount of baking powder added to mashed potatoes improves them. In measuring one-half cup butter, fill cup one-half full of water. Fill remaining space with butter.

When frying eggs, sprinkle one-half teaspoonful of flour in fat to prevent spattering.

Cold tea is a good fertilizer for house plants.

Tiny pieces of raw onion, green pepper and celery give a piquant flavor to mashed potatoes for variety's sake.

Boiled ham, corned beef and tongue should be returned to the water in which they were cooked until cold. It will give them much more flavor.

Buy grapefruit and oranges according to their weight, the heavier the better. Avoid thick skins, as this usually indicates that the fruit is dry and pulpy.

Add a tablespoon of borax to the water when washing light colored stockings that have become stained from shoes, and see how quickly the stains will wash out.

Dip the broom in a bucket of boiling water at least once a week. This will keep it clean and make it last much longer.

If a few drops of vinegar are added to the water in which eggs are to be poached, they will hold together and the white will not separate in the water. When cutting butter for the dinner table, if a piece of waxed paper is placed over the knife, you can cut butter in nice clean-cut squares.

To make sweet cream sour, to each cup of cream add 2 teaspoons of lemon juice, or, for evaporated milk, 1 teaspoon vinegar to each cup of milk.

The skin of a peach can be easily removed by placing the peach in a tablespoon and lowering it into fast boiling water for a few seconds. Skin will then easily peel off, without the fresh taste of the peach being affected.

Try to avoid discussions and disagreements at the dinner table. It is a known fact that better digestion follows a happy meal. Wives will find that husbands are more amenable with comfortably filled stomachs than during the process of eating.

AMOUNTS FOR SERVING 100 PERSONS

Meats

Three hams—about 45 pounds.

Thirty-five pounds of steak for Swiss steak.

Thirty-five pounds beef, fresh pork and salt pork for meat loaf.

Thirty-five pounds beef for pot roast.

Four chickens and 8 pounds veal for creamed chicken.

Eighteen pounds beef and 6 pounds veal for meat pie.

Forty pounds pork roast.

Vegetables

Three pecks potatoes.

Twelve cans peas.

Twelve pounds cabbage for salad.

Eleven cans beets for buttered beets.

Twenty-five pounds cabbage, 4 quarts milk and 3 packages grated cheese for Cabbage au Gratin.

Thirty-two cans corn, 1 dozen eggs and 1½ pounds of crackers for scalloped corn.

Six quarts cranberries.

Fruit Cocktail for 350

Five cans Black Bing cherries, 1 case (54) grapefruit, 12 cans pineapple, 6 cans apricots.

Miscellaneous

One pound coffee serves 40.

One quart cream serves 40.

One pound butter — 40 cubes.

One gallon ice cream serves 32.

One pound loaf sugar — 85 pieces.

Five loaves white bread and five loaves rye bread serves 100.

About 3 quarts whipping cream for dessert for 100.

Forty pounds apples for apple sauce for 100.

Ham & Woodthorts - chicken liver pâté - Bread dark
canapé - large potato chips - peanut butter - paprika